21ST-CENTURY
BLUE
Being a Bear in the Modern World

DAVID EDGAR
21ST-CENTURY
BLUE

Being a Bear in the Modern World

First published in Great Britain in 2010 by Derby Books Publishing Company Limited, 3 The Parker Centre, Derby, DE21 4SZ.

A catalogue record for this book is available from the British Library.

ISBN 978-1-85983-868-6
Printed and bound by Melita Press, Malta.

Contents

Dedication

For Thomas and Pauline Edgar. You can't choose your family, but even if I could, I'd still pick you.

Acknowledgements

When I started thinking about this book, my immediate reaction was that I wouldn't be able to do it. A combination of laziness and an inability to remember clearly – I drank a lot through most of this period – would see it fail to hit the Dickensian levels of literary genius I was expecting. The support of family and loyal friends made it happen.

A huge list of thanks await:

Firstly, to Chris Osborne and Scot van den Akker for listening to daily bulletins on the books progress and never allowing me to think it would be too much for me. Thanks for always being there.

To Alex Morton at DB Books for encouraging me.

To Robbie McKay for being my mate through the tough times and always listening.

To Stephen Smith and Mark Dingwall – two intellectual giants and good friends.

To Simon Leslie, Joanne Percival, Christine Sommerville, Fraser Martin, Gordon Dinnie, Cameron Bell and Andy Cumming at the RST.

To the Boyce brothers, Ian and Thomas. Good men and good mates.

To John Booth, Ian McColl and Stuart McColl. Blue to the core.

To Frances Porter for her inspirational emails.

To Alan Galloway for helping put me back together. I love you, man.

To Billy MacEwan for his example and, most of all, his friendship.

To all my various friends in fellowship. It's a special thing.

To Lisa McGregor for a glorious run and putting up with me in the face of extreme provocation.

To Sally McPherson for her kindness, love and support whenever I've needed it most. It's appreciated more than you know.

To all my extended family – what a cast of characters!

To Ann and Craig for their love and support.

To Cameron – the apple of my eye and my wee ray of sunshine.

And for my parents – you make me want to be a better person. I love you with all my heart.

celebrate a vibrant culture. We're not mainstream, we're punk rock. But the chances are, if you aren't one of us, you won't know that because it doesn't fit the stereotype and no one has bothered to look into it.

There has been so much written about Rangers fans over the last decade that someone will eventually have to open a library to host it all. But the thing that struck me is that for all the words available about us, very little has been written for us, and even less by us.

We've been poked, prodded, jostled, jeered. We've been encouraged to pay up and shut up. People have become so caught up in the cliché that they've stopped looking past it. We've been placed in a box and told to accept our role. Unfortunately for those who would wish us to simply take it and move on, we haven't been prepared to. This thing is more than the box you want to put us into.

That's what this book is for. This is the story of a young, handsome (clearly modest) man and his love for his club. It tells of some of the extraordinary situations a very ordinary fan has found himself in over the last decade in his role as spokesman for the largest independent Rangers Supporters' group in the world. It looks at what we are, where we came from and how we fit into the 21st century. It recalls some of the wonderful players and matches, and some of the Egil Ostenstad's. It talks about the press, it pokes fun at our rivals and it will, hopefully, give you a better idea of what it is to be a Teddy Bear these days.

Although being a Rangers fan is difficult, it's also fantastic. The spirit of the support, the humour, the history – it's special. I love being a Rangers man, which is a good job because I could no more stop being one than I could don a cape and fly. It was in my life before pretty much anything else, and it will be there until the day I shuffle off this mortal coil, no doubt lambasting the manager's formation or laughing at one of our great rivals' periodically comedic performances. This is a book for Rangers supporters like me.

I am a Rangers supporter – and I love it.

1

Born and Bred Blue

In the beginning, there was football.

I grew up in a town in North Ayrshire called Kilwinning. A beautiful little place with an abbey dating back to the 12th century, it's an area built on idiosyncrasies and folklore that is as loveable as it is mystifying to those who've never resided there. It was a reasonably harmonious town of around 20,000 inhabitants, with little serious crime, provided that you didn't count bevvy-induced affray as 'serious crime'. Nobody I knew did, anyway.

It's a town which comprises several housing schemes of age and quality. These are based around the main street, which is called 'Main Street' in an imaginative touch by the local forefathers; however, there is also a street called Gagarin Terrace, implausibly but wonderfully named after the Soviet cosmonaut, Yuri, who beat the Americans into space. I'd like to think that as he wrestled with his fears about the dangers of space travel, he was comforted briefly by the notion that one day he'd be immortalised in North Ayrshire.

I'm assuming that if you have had enough interest in the subject to actually pick up this book that you have some basic knowledge of Scottish society and the fact that, over the years, there's been a slight disagreement

Introduction

I am a Rangers supporter.

They're just five little words, but they have a myriad of connotations. To some it will mean that I am their brother in arms, someone who knows what it means to follow Scotland's premier football club. I am someone who understands that being a Rangers supporter means embracing a set of values, an ideal about how I should live my life, a belief system which moderates and affects my behaviour on a daily basis. To others it will mean that I subscribe to a set of values which embrace oppression, conservatism (with both a big and a small C) and intolerance. To others still it will mean that I quite like football and Rangers are the team I follow. And to a final section it will have as much meaning as saying that my favourite colour is red. Which it isn't. It's blue, obviously.

To the last two groups this book will most likely be something of a curiosity, a mildly diverting read in which a young man describes his adventures in a leisure pursuit. To the second group, pretty much anything I have written will be seized upon as yet more evidence that I have been at the forefront of a wide-ranging conspiracy. But the book, while intended for everyone – certainly in terms of sales, anyway – is primarily aimed at those in the first category, those hardy fellow travellers on the good ship Rangers FC.

Being a Rangers fan in the 21st century isn't easy. It's something which arrives with almost 140 years of baggage, most of it good, some of it not so. It sparks almost philosophical debates that encompass the age-old question 'What does it all mean?' Being a Rangers supporter means many things to many people, but the one thing that everyone agrees on is that it doesn't begin and end with the result on a Saturday, or a Sunday, or a Tuesday, or whatever strange time we kick-off these days to suit the TV companies.

Over the last decade Rangers supporters have found themselves on the end of press that would have made the Yorkshire Ripper feel a bit hard done by. We've been accused of being racist, sectarian, Neanderthal bigots who have rampaged all over the Continent like a pissed-up gang of modern-day Visigoths. We've been blamed by grandstanding politicians for some of Scotland's most complex and long-running social problems. We've witnessed organisations that have been set up and funded the government whose sole mission statement seems to be 'Rangers fans are bastards'. We've been sneered at in the press by people who've bought nice homes on the back of lambasting us. We've been portrayed as animals in expensive replica kits. And, on top of this, we've occasionally been rubbish on the pitch, which doesn't help.

The thing is, this isn't my experience of Rangers fans. In my time with the Rangers Supporters' Trust I've met literally hundreds, if not thousands, of Rangers fans. There are old and young, black and white, male and female. They have all been very different, but they have, in the main, been thoroughly decent human beings. They haven't fit into any conventional wisdom or set of rules about how they should look or act. The thing that has struck me most is their passion about their club. That is what they have in common – they are Rangers supporters and they care deeply about their club.

I know they've felt marginalised and voiceless. The huge growth in Rangers websites and social networks has partly been due to this. Rangers fans have been pushed closer together, and have turned inward to form and between Christians of different denominations. Many an interesting hour has been spent in rigorous intellectual discourse between Scottish followers of each faith as they made their case for why their belief system was more valid than the other. Or what really happened was that they pretty much just kicked the shit out of each other for a few centuries. The reason I mention this is that the two communities were represented by the two largest football teams in the country. Rangers was a club with a staunch Protestant heritage and Celtic had a Catholic background. This is pretty important in terms of the rest of the book making sense.

Kilwinning has a bit of a reputation in Scotland as an area that represents and celebrates Protestant hegemony. The rather simplistic idea is that Kilwinning is a hotspot of bigotry. This is not true. Kilwinning, especially in the 1980s, didn't have any sectarian tension at all due to the simple fact that it didn't have any Catholics. That's not 100 per cent true. There was an Italian man who ran Paul's Café, who most people assumed must have been Catholic, but he was foreign so it didn't really count. Then there was my Uncle Tam, who'd immigrated from nearby Stevenston to marry my Auntie Anne and whom everybody in the town loved. You still see Big Tam heading down to the Lemon Tree for a pint, and everybody in the town still loves him because he is such a wonderful and generous man. But he wasn't really religious and wasn't into football particularly, so he didn't seem particularly papish either. There was a chapel, subtly hidden away behind a housing estate and next to the railway, which most people felt probably existed for a reason but nobody you knew used. Therefore, sectarian tension didn't exist. You need two communities for a fight to develop.

Kilwinning has a very famous Masonic lodge in the Main Street. Lodges are numbered for identification, so you could belong to lodge number 1691, for a totally random example. Some research suggested that Kilwinning may have been home to the very first Masonic lodge in the world – imagine that! This exciting development caused a major stooshie, or fight for you non-Scots, as the number one had, somewhat predictably, **11** already been assigned. Being Kilwinning, the townspeople felt it very reasonable that every other lodge in the world simply move up one to let us claim our rightful place. The other lodges decided that this was, in fact, a bit of a pain in the arse and they weren't prepared to play along. With a breathtaking display of Kilwinning logic, which actually makes me so happy I could combust, they named their lodge nothing. As in '0'. Take that, number one!

I was, like most boys of my era, obsessed with football pretty much from the time I could walk. In those more innocent days, before the internet, games consoles and 600 channels in every home, parents were fervent believers in the idea that children should spend most of their existence outside the house. This strange custom – usually started with the words 'away out and play' – meant you had the freedom to do anything you wanted as long as it didn't involve straying too far from home or cost any money. Football, with its infinite capacity to cheaply entertain large gangs of kids for hours while simultaneously tiring them out, was God's gift to the parents who simply wanted peace after work to watch the telly.

In Kilwinning, everybody supported Rangers. It was endemic. The local junior (semi-pro) team was called Kilwinning Rangers, and the programme notes for their games often made no reference to their matches but would assess what had happened to the actual Rangers in the previous weeks. However, it was not a time of success for the men from Ibrox. In fact, 1965–85 had been disappointing overall, despite some of the wonderful players who had played for the club, such as Baxter, Brand, Millar, Johnstone, McLean, Stein, MacDonald, Smith and Cooper. This had been due to Celtic's best-ever team under Jock Stein, which contained players apparently all conceived and born in the centre circle at Parkhead. They won nine League titles in a row (and famously fluked a European Cup with an off-side goal, at a time when winning it only meant you had to play about three games, most of which you won by forfeit as the teams involved came from countries so small they didn't actually have any airlines and thus couldn't travel for the away leg. I'm not bitter).

Rangers rallied in the mid-1970s to win two trebles in three years under the management of the immortal Jock Wallace. This was before Aberdeen and Dundee United had arrived as a force in the late 1970s, thanks mainly to their managers. Aberdeen had the man who can rightly claim to be the greatest manager Scottish football has ever produced in Sir Alex Ferguson. He had a burning passion to defeat the Old Firm, some of which came from his experience at Ibrox as a player; Ferguson felt that he was badly treated by the club. Those who watched from the stands remember it was a more obvious reason – he was rubbish. Dundee United had Jim McLean, an odd little man who often looked as though he had recently eaten a lemon covered in dog piss. McLean was old-school Scottish football. He looked like the type of man who enjoyed farting in a lift and sneaking out. Actually, scratch that – he looked the type of man who enjoyed farting in a lift and then telling the rest of the people in it that he had done it. His Dundee United team were actually very good to watch, but I'm pretty sure the reason everyone in Scottish football laughed when United went down in 1995 was that they knew it would annoy him.

Rangers in the early 1980s were not really a team who would give you much reason to get excited. We had Davie Cooper, a truly wonderful footballer capable of doing things no one else could do. No less a judge than Ruud Gullit said Davie possessed the most cultured left foot of any footballer he'd shared a field with. However, Coop often seemed sucked down by the mediocrity around him, of which there was plenty. We had a young Ally McCoist, who at the time was not possessed of the swagger and cocksure certainty in his own ability that would see him end up with 355 goals for the club. As he fluffed the rare chances the midfield made for him, Ally simply didn't look like he was going to go down as the Rangers legend he did. There was a widespread and oft-mentioned belief that he couldn't hit a cow's arse with a banjo. Bobby Russell was a gifted midfielder who lacked that callous streak that someone like Gordon Strachan at Aberdeen possessed. You always got the impression that

Bobby could be a world-beater if only he believed it himself. And in terms of players to get you excited, that was about it.

The rest of the team tended to feature youngsters such as Dave McPherson, Gordon Dalziel and Ian Durrant or signings from other Scottish clubs who could best described as journeymen (Craig Patterson, Bobby Williamson, Cammy Fraser). My first striking hero was Iain Ferguson, a signing from Dundee who would actually go on to have a good career with Dundee United and Hearts but was not going to help propel Rangers past Celtic, never mind Aberdeen or Dundee United.

My earliest memories of football were of frustration. Simply put, it really wasn't supposed to be like that. We seemed incapable of putting a continued challenge in, and every time we built up a head of steam or a few decent results we'd invariably flop against some lowly non-entity like Clydebank. My big cousin, Alex, glory-hunting bastard that he is, had decided that he actually supported European Cup-winning Aberdeen and would mercilessly taunt me about Rangers' insipid form. (He switched back during the Souness era, which tells you something.) We won the League Cup a lot, which has the same status as the World Cup when you are six, but I could tell by the adults' reactions that it just wasn't enough. We were Rangers; we should be winning the League. It had been almost a decade since we had.

I say adults but, strangely, not my dad. Thomas Edgar was born in Londonderry, Northern Ireland, in the 1950s and arrived in Kilwinning in 1971 when the textile firm that employed him as a cutter sent him to work in the factory they had in the town. It was there he met my mum, Pauline Taggart, and decided to settle down.

My parents were, and are, forces of nature. I have never met anyone with their intelligence, pride, work ethic and sense of morality. They had two kids – me and my sister, Ann, born two years after me – and it was family first with them. My great gran lived with us, until she passed away, aged 97. My gran and papa (an Ayrshire word for grandad) lived at the bottom of the street. Various aunts and uncles lived within walking distance. We were a tight family unit.

And we had a lot of fun. My mum and dad didn't let Thatcher's Britain get them down. Their belief was that if you were fit, you worked, and they were fit. They didn't drink and they made sure their kids had all they needed and that we had a nice house, which wasn't the case for a lot of people I knew. They were always taking us out to places, spending time with us, making sure we knew we were loved. I've met people who came from houses that had 10 times the income of ours but a tenth of the love, and I wouldn't trade my mum and dad for anybody else's, though I've sometimes thought my mum would trade me for a BMW.

My old man was very conscious of the fact that, as a Northern Irish Protestant living in Kilwinning, he could easily be pigeon-holed by people's assumptions. He is not, as far as I know, a Mason. He is not a member of the Orange Lodge. He keeps his politics to himself. He didn't want to burden me with a series of his beliefs and watch me struggle against them. He wanted me to find out my opinions for and by myself. Ironically, I probably agree with him on most things these days, but I reached those decisions myself.

He taught me from an early age that the world is complex and your beliefs should not conform to an easy stereotype. You see it a lot in Scotland – 'I think this about this subject; therefore, I must think this about this other subject.' It's just a bit simplistic for me. I've voted in four elections now, and voted for each of the major parties at least once. Most issues I'm left-leaning, some right-leaning. I've never understood why all your views have to fit in one wee box.

Therefore, until the age of eight, I didn't know my dad was a Rangers fan. He would, when asked, proffer Brazil as his chosen side, which seemed fair, if a little impractical in terms of attending the matches. His annoyance was people in the town who would claim to be huge Rangers fans, have the tattoos and the tapes of Orange bands, but wouldn't know how to find Ibrox with a map and compass.

Another notion my Dad disabused me of at an early age was that the troubles in Northern Ireland were a valid subject for football fans to taunt each other about. We had family living there, among the ever-present fear of terrorism. To hear drunken idiots in Scotland talk about it with the gravitas of a child talking about a fight between Batman and Jaws – as if people dying in a tragic and debilitating civil war was something you could reduce to a football chant – was just wrong to us.

By the age of eight, with my room bedecked in red, white and blue, including a natty Rangers headboard, and my every free minute spent running about the back garden with my replica C.R. Smith jersey on, Dad was comfortable in the knowledge that he hadn't forced his team on me and I was now old enough to start attending matches. I say all this, but he could have been subconsciously influencing me by singing *The Bluebells are Blue* as I slept. It's the quiet ones you have to watch.

Everything was set. I was to make my first trip to Ibrox in November 1986, on the occasion of my ninth birthday. This had been a compromise with my Mum, who had wanted to wait until I was old enough to sit through the game without getting agitated. But as I now watched everything vaguely football-related on the telly, searched out highlight shows then taped them and watched them back endlessly, she had to concede that not only was I capable of sitting through 90 minutes, I probably could do so with more patience than most of the adults we knew.

Six months before that was to take place, the world went mental and Scottish football would never be the same again. A whirlwind with a perm and a moustache was about to blow through the country. His name was Graeme Souness.

Talking About a Revolution

In April 1986 my big cousin, Alex, phoned the house to tell me the news – Graeme Souness was going to be the new player-manager of Rangers. Graeme Souness! I remember sitting in the hall stunned, trying to take in the sheer mid-crushing enormity of what had happened.

Why the excitement? Apart from being Scotland's captain at a time when that meant something, Souness was plying his trade in Italy at Sampdoria. Before the advent of the internet and satellite television, Italian football seemed a million miles away, an exotic planet where all the best footballers in the world played. Nowadays I know more about who is eighth in Serie A than I do about who is second in the Scottish First Division, but back then it was mysterious and alluring. He had also been the captain and heartbeat of the Liverpool team of the late 1970s and early 1980s, which was pretty much universally lauded as the best team in the world. And he was coming to play for us!

I should also point out that I immediately trusted him, because he had a moustache. My dad has a moustache, as did all my uncles, as did every Northern Irish Protestant man I had ever met. Indeed, when I visit the wee country now, I am often disappointed by the younger generation's lack of facial hair. I have often wanted to grow a moustache, but I am ginger and camp enough as it is. Throw in a mouser and you are looking at the love-child of Freddie Mercury and Yosemite Sam.

Graeme Souness saved every single Rangers fan. That's a big statement, but I'd defy you to find 100 season-ticket holders who were about then who would deny it. He took our club, the wonderful old institution, and he improved it. He was a disciplinarian, and Rangers fans love disciplinarians. Celtic fans often accuse us of being ruthlessly pragmatic in our approach to the game and harp on about the 'Celtic Way', a mythical style of cavalier football that they are apparently world famous for. We, on the other hand, apparently play football in the style of strategically-placed cannons, trying to deflect the ball towards the opposition goal through sheer brute force. A cursory look through Rangers' history will show this is not true, however, by unearthing some wonderful ball players. In my time watching the 'Gers, we have had Cooper, Durrant, Wilkins, Walters, Steven, Mikhailichenko, Laudrup, Gascoigne, Albertz, McCann, Ferguson, van Bronckhorst, Amato, de Boer, Mols, Caniggia, Arveladze, Buffel and Davis. These are players of craft and guile, not the hammer-throwers of lore.

Yes, we've also had guys who could mix it a bit. You need that. Every successful team has to have a balance. One only needs to look at Kevin Keegan's Newcastle team of the 1990s or Arsene Wenger's current Arsenal team. They're all very pretty, all very nice to watch, but they win nothing. Football is not ice-skating; you don't get points for style. Yes, it's nice to watch good football, but in the end it's all about how many big silver things you wave at your fans that matters.

This was the case when predictably tiresome arguments emerged between Old Firm fans on their sides' respective runs to the UEFA Cup Finals of 2003 and 2008 – who had had the better season? Removing all subjective arguments, it surely comes down to who won the most trophies in those years. In 2003 Celtic won nothing as Rangers recorded a domestic clean sweep. In 2008 Rangers won both domestic Cups. Rangers, surely, had the better season when they reached the UEFA Cup Final. But Celtic had 'beaten better teams'. This is absolutely unprovable, yet that's what we heard. It also ignores the fundamental issue of all Cup competition; you can only beat the teams you are drawn against.

One walloper from the dark side even claimed that because Celtic had lost 3–2 in their Final after extra-time, this was better than Rangers' normal-time 2–0 defeat. It's tough to know where to start with that one, but a 3–2 defeat is still a defeat. You win the same – nothing.

Celtic's fans then claimed the moral high ground. Porto had only beaten them due to their diving and time-wasting antics. Celtic were the moral champions. Obviously, in houses from Reykjavik to Rio, people were shaking their heads in dismay at their TV and saying 'I refuse to acknowledge Porto as the winners of this match. Celtic are, in my mind, the UEFA Cup winners of 2003, damn the result!'

Anyone would be permitted a wry smile at being asked to feel sorry for Martin O'Neill's team of divers, thugs and Henrik Larsson. Porto didn't need to dive because Celtic had players such as Mjallby, Balde and Valgaeren, who were to discreet tackling what Katie Price is to quiet dignity. Celtic were effective at what they did, and did it very well, but for anyone to suggest that this most streetwise of teams had lost to some foreign chicanery is either sweetly naïve to the point of simplicity or a bit mental. Celtic lost to Porto because Porto were better at football than they were. Rangers lost to Zenit St Petersburg for exactly the same reason. We had two trophies to help ease the pain. Celtic had none.

To me, whenever you start getting into the realms of 'moral' victories and how they matter more than real ones, you are on a slippery slope. I have never seen Rangers lose a football match in actuality but win it morally; I have seen us lose somewhat unfortunately, I have seen us lose because of scandalous refereeing decisions, and I have seen us lose because we were rubbish or the other team were just plain better. The bottom line is that we lost. How you play isn't important, it's whether you win that counts.

Souness realised this and immediately did the thing every sensible manager does: he built from the back. He brought in Terry Butcher, the England captain when Bryan Robson was injured, which he always was, and Chris Woods, the England goalkeeper when Peter Shilton was injured, which he never was. These signings were huge. English players didn't move to Scotland; it was the other way round. Always had been. But Souness wasn't going to let convention dictate his future. He was a winner, and any team he managed was damn well going to win too.

What these signings did was imbue the support with a feeling of intense excitement. Season tickets sold out immediately. Scottish Football was being talked about all over the UK for the first time in years. English clubs had been banned from Europe after the Heysel stadium disaster, and this meant that the only European football of note in the British Isles would be played north of Hadrian's Wall. Players at the top English clubs suddenly became aware of the choice they had if they wanted to test themselves at the top level – the south side of Glasgow or abroad. Rangers suddenly became very attractive. And we had the Souness factor.

Rangers lost Souness' first game, which was away to Hibs, and the media went mental. Souness had been sent off for what at the time I felt was a slightly mis-timed tackle but, looking back, was actually a fantastically brutal assault on Hibs player George McCluskey (an ex-Celtic player who'd scored the winning goal against us in the 1980 Cup Final – I could hardly sleep that night with concern for him). It sparked a 21-man brawl. Only Hibs 'keeper Alan Rough stayed out of it. Having met Roughy a few times since, I suspect he couldn't be arsed running halfway up the park in the summer heat.

Souness' first game at Ibrox was also my first game. We went 2–0 up against Dundee United, and we were playing really well. Jim McLean's pissy-lemon face was in full effect, it was sunny, I was happy and my dad bought me a hot dog. This was magic.

And eventually, we got beaten 3–2. Bastards.

I don't remember all that much about it apart from the immensity of Ibrox and the noise. I'd never heard anything like it. It was a throaty roar, an enormous, gut-moving wall of growl and cheer, which seemed to emerge any time anything happened. People sang, clapped and swore. It was even better than it was on the telly. From a child of the 1980s there is no higher praise.

Souness was everything you want in a Rangers manager. Like Jose Mourinho, he talked the talk but walked the walk. There's nothing worse for opposition fans than a manager who talks shit but can back it up. That was Souey. People accused him of being arrogant, and he was. And so he bloody well should have been. He'd won everything he could as a player, had played in the World Cup Finals and now he was managing one of the biggest clubs in the world.

We won the League that year, as Celtic imploded and Aberdeen had to come to terms with losing Ferguson to Manchester United. We played some superb stuff and seemed to sign a player every quarter of an hour or so. There were queues at the ticket office for entry to League matches. There was, as in football parlance, a buzz about the place.

There was the backline featuring Woods in goal and a centre-back partnership of Souness and the rock-hard figure of Graham Roberts, a Cockney who seemed to take great pleasure in winding up the opposition. Next there was Butcher, with his tenacious defending and ability to hit 60-yard passes with the unerring accuracy of a missile-launcher. Jimmy Nicholl, the stylish Northern Irish right-back who always seemed to have a bit of time on his hands to comfortably thwart any attack down his flank, followed and Stuart Munro came at left-back. Munro had cost £15,000 from Alloa in the wilderness years and was never the best player, but that year he seemed to grow in the exalted company around him.

Midfield saw Souness pair up youngsters Derek Ferguson and Ian Durrant. Ferguson, older brother of Barry, was actually the best player of the family, but a penchant for the high-life and inability to get on with the boss did for him. Durrant was sublime. The nearest modern player to him is Paul Scholes, but Durrant was as good, if not better. He had finesse, guts and an uncanny ability to get into the box just as it mattered, like me arriving at the bar when it is someone else's round. You can't teach that; it just comes naturally. It's a gift.

Coop was on the wing and had seemed reborn that season. He tore Ilves Tampere of Finland apart at Ibrox in the UEFA Cup with a display so mesmeric you could have set it to music and called it ballet. He scored goals, he beat players and we sang *Davie Cooper on the Wing*. He was astonishing.

Up front Coisty was rattling the cow with the banjo consistently. He'd been joined by youngster Robert Fleck, a strange looking young man who resembled a potato that had been in a nasty car crash. But he knew where the back of the net was, and the goals flowed. It was a heady time.

It wasn't all fun in 1986–87. In January 1987 we lost at home in the Cup to bottom-of-the-table Hamilton Academical. We absolutely battered them but couldn't score. Chris Woods broke the world record for minutes without losing a goal that day. I still remember the programme saying 'The women will have been wondering why the men are talking about clean sheets all of a sudden', a piece of quality sexism you wouldn't get away with today. He was beaten by Adrian Sprott near the end and we were out. It was a sore one but no catastrophe given the rest of the year. We had a wonderful team, a wonderful manager and an incredible home.

Ibrox was one of the few stadiums in the UK that was all-seated at the time, a result of the Ibrox disaster of 1971. It was an horrific event that the UK authorities steadfastly refused to learn from, pathetically reducing the magnitude of the tragedy by maintaining that it happened at an Old Firm game and those were legendarily intense, as if the strips the players wore mattered one iota. It took Hillsborough for the rest of the country to realise something Rangers had understood immediately, that football fans should not be risking their lives when attending matches. The stadium which stands today is a memorial to the 66 who died that day, which is why I hate the pathetic maintenance it has suffered from during David

Murray's last 10 years as 'custodian'. To me, it is the equivalent of allowing the Cenotaph to fall into disrepair. Every time we enter that stadium we honour those who died in our memory.

It would be remiss of me not to mention possibly the single most mental game I've ever had the good fortune to witness: Rangers versus Celtic in October 1987, before the arrival of Murray. That this match ended in a draw is the most mundane thing about it. Within the opening 10 minutes there was a clash between Chris Woods and Celtic striker Frank McAvennie, Butcher and Roberts also getting involved. It was, looking back, a bit of a nothing incident, but the atmosphere at Old Firm games back then caused sensible men to do strange things. Woods, Butcher and McAvennie were all red-carded during the 2–2 game and the trio – along with Roberts – had to answer charges of 'behaviour likely to cause a breach of the peace' in a court case that followed. Woods and Butcher had McAvennie by the throat, and McAvennie seemed to lash out back. Sensible refereeing would have seen the skirmish over inside 30 seconds, but not this time. The ref sent everyone off, and Graham Roberts had to go in goal for us. He achieved infamy by conducting the crowd in a rousing version of *The Sash*. Woods and Butcher were later convicted and fined, Roberts got a 'not proven' (meaning 'we think you did it but we're not sure') and McAvennie got away scot-free. It's a conspiracy!

We absolutely romped the League that year, and although no one could possibly know it, this would be the start of Rangers' nine-in-a-row title success. I've given away what happens there a wee bit, but again I am trusting that if you have got this far you probably know the main events in Scottish football in this era. Unless you are a reviewer and you are reading this because you have to. In which case, may I sympathise. You have a very difficult job to do, and I personally feel you do it rather well. Can I also say your hair looks lovely today, and I've always felt that shade brings out your eyes.

Celtic had over-achieved in 1987–88, which became apparent in 1988–89 when they fell apart. Aberdeen had a decent side, but it was becoming clear that with the huge sums of money Rangers were spending – and more importantly, generating – it would be very difficult to match us over the course of a whole season. Richard Gough had arrived from Spurs and was simply the complete defender. There was literally nothing the big man wasn't good at. Roberts had been sold after a spat with the manager. This was Souness at his belligerent finest. After an end-of-season clash with Aberdeen had ended in a single-goal defeat, Souness told Roberts the goal had been his fault. Roberts reacted angrily, one word followed another, and it ended with Roberts telling the boss, 'If that's how you feel, then maybe you should sell me.' Souness simply replied, 'Consider yourself sold.' And that's what happened. No matter how good he'd been, or how much the fans loved him, he'd crossed Souness and Souness was the man. I loved that. None of this wishy-washy crap or 'sitting down with the player to get it sorted'. No, a metaphorical swift kick to the balls and then off – that's how you do business.

We famously spanked Celtic 5–1 early that season, and the only regret Rangers fans who witnessed that match will have is that it could and probably should have been double figures. Celtic actually scored first, but then Rangers destroyed them. Ray Wilkins scored a fantastic goal, a dipping volley from 20 yards that commentator Jock Brown described as 'a goal made in England'. There was still 20 minutes left when we'd reached five, and Souness brought himself on. Unfortunately, he'd decided to bring himself on to slow the pace down and take the piss out of the opposition. Normally I'd be all for that in an Old Firm game, but in this instance Souness had misread the crowd. We wanted to absolutely annihilate them, and we very much could have that day. In the end they got away with a battering rather than a full-blown deconstruction. Disappointed after a 5–1 win against our biggest rivals? A wee bit. Welcome to the world of the Rangers fan.

Everything in the garden was rosy. The summer would bring more signings. It must have been a heady time to be a football journalist. We were always close to signing someone, spying on another, linked with this player or that. I remember a story in the *Glasgow Evening Times* one night linking us with Michel Platini. It was complete bollocks, of course, but that was the thing; it could have been true. Anything seemed possible for Rangers. I'll give Souness his due, however. That summer of 1989 he made a signing that was even more unbelievable than the signing of the world's best player. He made a signing whose impact would reverberate around Scottish football for a decade. He signed, from right under Celtic's noses, the most controversial player available: Maurice Johnston.

3

Stealing Celtic's Mojo

Rangers FC had a singular, unwritten signing policy in their history up until 1989: we didn't really sign Catholics. Note the way I've written that. We didn't not sign Catholic players per se, but we didn't exactly clamber over other teams to get them. We had a young guy at the time called John Spencer who was a Catholic, for example, and we had had other players in our history, but it was pretty much a given that we didn't exactly have a squad packed full of players of that background.

Had it held us back? It would be impossible to argue that it hadn't had an effect. Scotland is a small place, and when you voluntarily reduce the player pool available to you, you limit the amount of room for manoeuvre. Celtic had signed Protestant players – though there was no chance of anyone who wasn't Catholic invading their board room – but this had allowed them to get players such as Danny McGrain and Kenny Dalglish, whom even the most blinkered Rangers fan would have to concede were wonderful players. (It also allowed them to sign guys like Jim Melrose, but they were welcome to him.)

It sounds shocking to modern ears, but that was the way it had been back then and up to that point. Certain players were passed over by Rangers. How deep-seated was this discrimination? It's tough to say. Alex Ferguson remembers Willie Waddell recommending a young player to him when he was St Mirren's manager with the words 'He's not right for us, but he's very good,' which Ferguson took to mean he was a Catholic. The player, Frank McGarvey, went on to play for Liverpool and Celtic. That distills the strangeness of the situation for me – Waddell wouldn't sign him but went out of his way to try to further his career elsewhere. There's a contradiction at the heart of that story which belies the unmanageability of the whole situation.

I've heard Rangers fans argue vehemently that there was no policy, and I'd agree with that to a point. It wasn't an official club strategy, put in place and handed down to employees as part of the code of practice. However, you have to look at the situation dispassionately and admit that there had to be something there.

Souness had said repeatedly that he wasn't interested in the arguments; he would sign players he felt were good enough, regardless of creed or colour. He had signed Mark Walters, a fantastically gifted black winger, from Aston Villa and he'd been a revelation. Walters was immediately a crowd favourite at Rangers; skilful, pacy and with an eye for goal, he soon became an integral part of the set-up at Ibrox. Walters also deserved credit for the strength of character he displayed in his first few months in Scotland; he suffered some of the most disgraceful racial abuse witnessed north of the border when he made his debut against Celtic in January 1988. Monkey noises were prevalent and bananas were thrown as he warmed up. Celtic substitute Gerry Britton later said he had been shocked at the sheer volume of fruit thrown.

Souness had a young, ambitious chairman. Actually, he was also the owner. David Murray was a friend of Souness and had bought the club for £6 million in November 1988. Murray was an effervescent young multi-millionaire, who'd overcome losing both legs in a car accident as a young man to build a successful empire in the steel business. Tempted by the prestige the club offered him, he invested. He wasn't an absentee owner by any stretch of the imagination; Murray was a constant presence around the club and did a lot for Rangers, certainly in the first 10 years of his ownership. We'll come to the second decade later.

One of Murray's most spectacularly successful cons was to create the impression he'd taken Rangers from a status akin to Raith Rovers when he took over in November 1988. He most certainly did not. The Souness Revolution, as it came to be known, was led by David Holmes, a man who has been deliberately and unforgivably airbrushed from history by his successor as chairman. It was Holmes who had the vision to go for Souness, Holmes who led us out of the wilderness and made Rangers the attractive proposition it was to a young David Murray in 1988. His place in the Ibrox pantheon of greats is assured but considerably underplayed.

I've said some nasty things about David Murray before and, rest assured, I'll be saying a lot more later, but he does deserve credit for his initial decade at Rangers. He had attempted to buy Ayr United, his boyhood club, but had been rebuffed. I've heard people say that the seaside club's fans must deeply regret their then-board's decision to chase Murray's offer, but as I watched Lloyds Bank sink their claws deeper and deeper into Rangers I wondered if that was true.

Murray was an Edinburgh boy and not particularly fond of Glaswegians, demonstrating the attitude those from Scotland's second city tend to possess. He found some of the outdated practices that were enshrined at Ibrox to be somewhat backwards, and he was firmly behind his manager's moves to widen Rangers employment diversity policy. They had stated that religion would not be a barrier to them when going for a player. Given the nature of the two men involved and their personalities, it would be naïve in the extreme to suggest that they didn't fancy the idea of being the men who would go down in history for ending this signing policy; regardless of their motivations, they made the alterations.

Speculation had been rife that Souness was close to signing Glasgow-born Republic of Ireland midfielder Ray Houghton from Oxford, but he eventually ended up at Liverpool. Even so, it was an indicator that Souness was serious about signing a high-profile Catholic player. It seemed just a matter of time. But the one he got couldn't have been more high profile.

Maurice Johnston was the poster boy of the Celtic support. He was the archetypal glamorous star striker – blonde hair, earring, the ability to score vital goals. He was a dyed-in-the-wool Celtic man too, having grown up supporting them. After a successful spell in England with Watford, where he'd played in the 1984 FA Cup Final, he'd returned to Scotland and played very well for them. Celtic were, however, run by a board comprised of two families, the Kellys and the Whites. It had ever thus been so. They were in charge, and they were so parsimonious in the wages they paid that many a Celtic player felt compelled to try to earn what they were worth elsewhere. Johnston was the same and headed off to Nantes in France in 1987. However, this was not before the memorable Skol League Cup Final of 1986, in which Rangers defeated Celtic 2–1, the winner coming from a hotly-disputed late penalty awarded for a foul by Roy Aitken on Terry Butcher. Davie Cooper duly dispatched it, we won the Cup and Celtic imploded. Johnston was sent off in the final minutes. To wind up the Rangers fans, he blessed himself as he walked up the tunnel. It's safe to say, however, that we did not expect to ever see Mo in the light blue, especially as we chanted 'Mo, Mo, f**k your Mo, f**k your Maurice Johnston' at him.

The thing about Johnston was he was already a good player before he moved, but he had improved dramatically abroad. In those days there wasn't wall-to-wall European football on TV, so his progress could only be judged accurately when he returned to play for Scotland. He scored a double in a famous win against France at Hampden in 1989 on a filthy night, and he ran the French defence ragged. He also linked superbly with Ally up front. But still, it was all academic to a Rangers fan. He'd played for Celtic. You didn't play for both.

That has changed, of course. Several players have done so recently. Celtic had Steven Pressley and Mark Brown. This left a slightly sour taste but was easy enough to cope with because Brown had been a reserve **29** 'keeper at Ibrox and Pressley is, well, Pressley. He could well be the least sympathetic character in Scottish football. Witness his comment as Falkirk manager that 'everybody wants to see this club relegated.' Yes — because of him. No one I know, no matter which team they follow, has ever had anything against Falkirk. Until Pressley became their boss and started talking out of his arse.

There is also the strange case of Kenny Miller. Kenny joined Rangers from Hibs in 2000 as one of the most exciting young Scots to emerge in years. It didn't quite happen for him and he was off to Wolves in 2001, where he did quite well and became a Scotland favourite due to his selfless running. In 2006, however, he joined Celtic on a Bosman. It's understandable; football is a job and he was offered, from a career point of view, a tremendous opportunity. It stuck in the throat of Rangers fans, but what did he care? Especially when he scored his first Celtic goal against us and celebrated like he'd just scored the winning goal in a World Cup Final.

It then went sour for Kenny at Parkhead and he left for Derby County, though their inevitable relegation from the Premiership seemed to suggest he'd be on his bike again soon enough. Rumours started emerging that Walter Smith, having worked with him with the Scotland team, wanted to bring him back to Ibrox. The Rangers fans reacted to this with a united message. The Cup Final of 2008 heard the massed banks of Bears singing 'You can stick your Kenny Miller up yer arse' with gusto. I described him to a newspaper as a 'deeply unpopular signing'. I wasn't going out on a limb with that one. We didn't want him.

He came back, and he did well, working hard, scoring goals and eventually winning round all but the most ardent of his critics. That said, I still have friends who dislike him intensely and can't get past the whole Celtic thing. When he scored the winner in the 2010 League Cup Final against St Mirren I'm pretty sure my friend Stevie was in the stadium long after the place emptied, waiting on extra-time because he doesn't recognise goals Miller scores as counting. Stevie's hardcore.

It's a tough one. Logically, you should be able to play for both. Managers should be free to sign whomever they feel will help improve their team. But, cards on the table, I'd rather people didn't. If you've played for one side of the Old Firm, it should pretty much rule you out of playing for the other. There's nothing worse than someone you used to idolise – or at least like – strutting about in the colours of your greatest rivals. This isn't unique to us. Sir Alex Ferguson point-blank refused to sell Gabriel Heinze to Liverpool because it was Liverpool. You've made your bed, now lie in it.

But this was a question for science-fiction writers back then, so far away did it seem. Celtic announced a deal to bring back Johnston from France in summer 1989, even parading him in their new strip at a Parkhead. It was a serious signal of intent from the club that they wanted to try to regain the title they had just lost, especially as their board's usual idea of pushing the boat out in terms of spending was to order an extra bottle of sherry for the Christmas party. While I wouldn't say Rangers fans were exactly panicking, it definitely gave us something to think about in terms of the next season.

Maybe you've won the lottery. Perhaps you've taken a Ryanair flight which left on time. Those events are, I grant you, surprising, but I guarantee you nothing could add up to the sense of mind-blowing bewilderment that ripped through me when I saw the front page of *The Sun* that said 'MO SIGNS FOR 'GERS!'

It wasn't so much that Rangers had signed a Catholic as the one that they had signed. Not only was he an ex-Celtic player, a Celtic pin-up, but he'd apparently been a Celtic player a month before. There had been rumours and whispers that the deal was in trouble, but no one in their right mind would have thought he would sign for us.

Certain sections of the press still like to peddle the idea that thousands of angry Protestants marched on Ibrox, torches burning, demanding that war be declared. 'Scarves were burned in protest!' they said. Yet the footage on the news at the time showed a couple of rough guys, who'd clearly been hauled out of the stadium bar by the news teams, burning suspiciously new-looking scarves at a location that just happened to be perfect for film crews. Look at the footage on YouTube or watch the reports from the 20th anniversary of the signing – it's the same two guys, every time. This utterly random and in no way orchestrated event was used as proof that the Rangers support were against Johnston. 'Season tickets were returned!' was another line trotted out. Maybe some were, but they were like gold dust at the time. I have no doubts that they were sold again pretty quickly.

That's not to suggest everyone was over the moon about the whole thing. It had been a very clever move by Souness though. Sections of the support were upset at what they saw as an attack on the club's traditions, but this had to be balanced with the knowledge that it really, really upset the Tims. Death threats, letters to Pope John Paul II demanding Mo be excommunicated, people renaming their first born from 'Maurice' to 'Declan' – it was a crazy time.

John Brown told a great story at an RST Dinner of Mo arriving at Rangers' Italian training camp at Il Ciocco to meet the rest of the players. As a wind-up, the squad got a single small table and set it up in the corner of the room with one place setting on it. When Johnston walked in, a deathly silence fell over the dining area and the players refused to look up. Johnston saw the table in the corner and headed over to it. He turned and said, 'You lot are nothing but a bunch of dirty Orange bastards,' to which Ian Ferguson replied, 'Aye, and don't you f****ing forget it.' Tension suitably broken, Johnston fitted in and played very well almost from the start.

Johnston's most famous goal was his injury-time winner against Celtic in November 1989. He'd been a bit hopeless that day, to be honest. He'd missed several chances against a constant background of some intolerable abuse from the Celtic support in the Broomloan Stand, but when he side-footed home the only goal and ran to the Copland, that was it. He'd been accepted for what he was first and foremost – a very good footballer.

Those who have crossed the divide, so to speak, are referred to as having 'jumped the dykes' in Glasgow, sleeping with the enemy, so to speak. It's difficult for fans to get their heads around it. Given the antipathy between the two clubs and their supporters, it's impossible for us on the terraces to understand how someone could do that. I remember when Paul Lambert, a boyhood Rangers fan, crashed a beauty in against us for Celtic in a 2–0 defeat at Parkhead in 1998. He ran towards the hooped hordes triumphantly as the place went wild, and those of us in the away end looked collectively like someone had stolen our dog. How could he do it? How could he score for them against us? Why would he even want to?

It comes down to the harsh but undeniable truth that footballers and fans are a different breed nowadays. The era of guys playing for the club because they loved it is gone. Football is a huge business, the players well-remunerated executives. The bond between player and supporter has been eroded by the chasm in lifestyles. Almost every player at Ibrox will earn more in a month than I do in a year. Most of them would be off if someone offered to increase their already massive wage. I, and every other supporter at every other club, will be there until we choose to stop going or, in truly hopeless cases like mine, die. They don't care as much as we do. Why should they? It's a job to them, nothing more. American business writer Daniel Pink suggested in his book *Drive* that as soon as money comes into play, any activity ceases to be fun and starts to be work. It's a basic human psychological tenet. Therefore, Lambert was doing exactly what he was paid to do. I can't blame him for providing for his family, especially as, given his interviews, he was unlikely to find employment in many other places.

Fans always say, when asked, that they could never sign for the opposition, but it's a redundant question. You are not the person you would be if you were a footballer, especially one good enough to play for one half of the Old Firm. Think about it. Footballers are told from the age of about 10 how special they are, how they need to be utterly determined to make it. They don't watch matches because they are too busy playing in their own. They become fans of themselves rather than teams. They have to. Football is a brutal, cruel business, devoid of sentimentality. Those who make it have to be skilful and talented, but they also have to be ruthlessly single-minded.

I was once asked on the radio if I would wear a Celtic top for charity. Frankly, I wouldn't wear a Celtic top for a blow-job. Off Kate Moss. While she threw money at me. I realise some people will be judging me on that, but I can live with it. The point of doing that is to make you look like a good guy, someone who is above all the petty rivalries, someone who realises that it's just a game. I'm not that guy. If I had done that, it would be to try to prove to the Celtic supporters listening what a lovely bloke I was. They'd still have thought I was a wanker. Why? Because I support Rangers. This is how this works. Roma fans don't parade in Lazio tops, Manchester United fans are rarely seen cutting about in Liverpool strips. Only in Glasgow does football rivalry automatically become bigotry. (I donated the money to the charity myself in the end. You could say I paid £250 for the privilege of not wearing a Celtic top. I still think it was a bargain.)

On the 20th anniversary of Johnston's transfer, various media outlets ran pieces about the move. It was clear that some couldn't forgive and forget and, to be honest, I understand that. It was a betrayal. Souness said that the deal had caused Celtic such psychological damage that it effectively took them the best part of a decade to get over it. McNeill said that he'd felt Souness only pursued the deal to inflict more pain on Celtic. He's probably right, but then that's how business works. You try to get ahead in any way that you can.

What it did do was usher in the era of true diversity at Rangers. We've had a rainbow coalition pretty much since then, and no one bats an eyelid at a players' background now. One of the most popular players of recent years is Madjid Bougherra, an Algerian Muslim. Nacho Novo is welcome to have a beer in any Rangers fan's house until the day he dies due to his work rate and his love of the club. I've never heard anyone mention his religion. Neil McCann was a West of Scotland Catholic who was loved because he had great ability and a knack of playing well in big games. It's been the breakthrough people hoped for when Johnston put pen to paper.

When Rangers bought Johnston, many in the media claimed they had 'forced' Rangers to do it. Gerry McNee in particular used to take great credit for it. Rangers had been told that to become a truly universal club, they had to 'shed the bigoted image'. This was the mantra, the perennial war cry of those who loved putting the boot into the club under the banner of social progress. You must sign a Catholic, they demanded. And then we did, and they still moaned. No matter what we did, we couldn't 'shed the bigoted image'. It took me years to figure out that we couldn't shed it because it was them who had given us it.

But all that was a while away. My first real love affair was about to come to an end. Souness packed his bag, retouched his perm and headed back to Liverpool.

4

Goodbye Graeme

The 1990s arrived with Rangers so far ahead of Celtic it was embarrassing, or at least it would have been if we weren't so busy taunting them about it. I was fortunate enough to witness possibly the best team I have ever seen in the flesh around this time. Sadly, it wasn't us but Red Star Belgrade, who knocked us out of the European Cup in 1990. I say knocked us out, but that doesn't really do it justice. They did to us what a cat does to a bird – much toying before an inevitable and savage conclusion. It wasn't that we had a bad team – far from it – but with Prosinecki and Pancev in their squad we just couldn't get near them. Prosinecki apparently smoked 60 fags a day. I shudder to think how good he'd been if he could actually run.

The only cloud on the horizon was the growing detachment of Graeme Souness. There wasn't the same fire in his belly that there had been when he'd first arrived. I think it was a facial hair issue; he'd traded in the mouser for a full beard, skillfully shaved to the same designer length every day. I didn't like it then, and I don't like it now. Beards are for people with something to hide and Brian Blessed. Unless you have something to hide or are Brian Blessed, you should stick to the mouser.

However, this portentous sign was missed by most of the commentators as Souness grew ever more frustrated in Scotland.

In truth, Scottish football wasn't big enough for him. The pettiness, the parochialism, the sheer undiluted small-minded narkiness of the whole set-up wore him down. There was a famous incident when a St Johnstone tea-lady had a go at him for some perceived slight before a match in Perth. She was all over the newspapers, posing with a tea-cup, and people revelled in the arrogant Rangers manager 'meeting his match' in the fearsome Aggie, scourge of Souness. We've never been shot of the old cow since, as she periodically popped up every time we were due to play St Johnstone. We have very low standards for celebrity in Scotland. Again, she was pictured with a tea-cup, obviously because most readers would have been unable to understand that she was a tea-lady without this enormous visual clue.

(Incidentally, St Johnstone love nothing more than to prove how 'street' they are than by thumbing their nose at actual celebrities. Their most famous fan is Ewan McGregor, who was attending a match at McDiarmid Park and was subsequently refused entry to the boardroom because he wasn't wearing a tie. Being a classy guy, he simply moved on with his friends. I mention this because I want him to play me in the film version of the book. We look very similar.)

Then there was the infamous tunnel incident. Souness had been banned from the dug-out for a few matches, and had been caught on camera standing in the tunnel at Ibrox when technically he wasn't allowed to. Scottish Television seemed to take great pleasure in sending the footage to the SFA, and Souness' ban was subsequently increased.

This was all having an effect on Souness, who grew ever more frustrated and tetchy. He dropped and sold Terry Butcher before a League Cup semi-final at Hampden, feeling that Butcher was past his best (he was probably right). However, it was a shabby way for Butcher's Ibrox career to end. His service had earned him the right to leave with his head held high, and it was a mistake on Souness's part to deny him that. It also seems to have left a mark on Butcher, who has managed to become one of the Rangers support's least favourite sons during his subsequent years in Scotland due to his comments on the club.

The real sign that it was all getting to Souness came after an incident with Gerry McNee, erstwhile Scottish sport reporter and STV stalwart. You could always feel Gerry before you could see him on *Scotsport*, a huge, malevolent presence at the corner of your screen. Gerry forever looked like he'd rather be selling his bottom at the top of Sauchiehall Street to make a living than working in what he called the 'cesspit' of Scottish football. This did, obviously, beg the question, why didn't he simply sod off and give everyone else peace?

Billy McNeill had infamously punched him during an altercation a decade before. Finally, something I can get onside with 'Caesar' for. Souness *threatened* him on a flight back from Bucharest after McNee had been upset that Souness had given information to a rival organisation. Apparently, Gerry found this unfair. It never crossed his mind that Souness may simply just have not liked him. Souey uttered the immortal words 'Billy McNeill punched you and you got back up. I'll punch you and you won't get back up.' McNee screamed about it forever and a day afterwards. Souness was wrong. He shouldn't have threatened to punch him. Can I just say for the record that you should never punch Gerry McNee. Not unless you are too drunk to kick him.

On top of all of this Souness started getting a wee bit of stick from the crowd for the first time due to leaving out fans' favourite Ally McCoist. They didn't get on all that well, Souness thinking McCoist a bit of a smart-arse. Coisty was, however, a god in Govan, and the fans didn't take too kindly to seeing him on the bench every week, especially when he would come on and generally score.

At the beginning of the 1990–91 season Souness had splashed out £1 million on Mark Hateley. Big Attila would go on to legend status, but for the first six months he wasn't much cop. To be fair, he'd been blighted by injuries for the previous couple of seasons and was still finding his feet at his new club, but when he was established as the number-one striker, with Johnston his regular partner, fans gave him a hard time. It's a credit to him that he kept plugging away until he won the fans over.

This takes us off on an interesting tangent – how demanding Rangers fans are. We really are, it cannot be denied. Players generally have to make a blistering start to their Ibrox career to be in with a chance of acceptance. Anything less than brilliant sees a player marked 'pish'. Once saddled with that, you have one hell of an uphill climb to turn it around. We're quick to judge and long to change our minds.

I've heard people say that it's a consequence of the modern world that people make up their minds instantly these days and nothing gets time to settle. In music, for instance, if a band doesn't deliver a classic or a big-seller with their first album, the chances are they will be dropped by their label, as opposed to the old days when they'd be given several albums to mature into a decent act. I'm not sure I believe that; Rangers crowds have been like this since I started going and, my dad assures me, were like that long before, too.

I don't necessarily think this is a bad thing. We don't accept failure and we don't like second-rate players. We want to be the best, so we demand the best. However, we can take it too far. Some of the abuse dished out to Rangers players by the home crowd would be deemed unacceptable if it had come from the away end. Charlie Adam was a case in point. Charlie was possessor of a rather cultured left foot, but his fitness and positional sense was often called into question. He took pelters from our own support for the crime of not being Ryan Giggs. There is nothing wrong in being critical, but it's when to do it that prompts the debate. For me, the place to do it is before and after the match, never during.

While frustration can play a big part in it, the only time it is truly acceptable to get on the back of a player is if he appears to be giving less than 100 per cent. If he's continually trying his best but not delivering the performance level required, then it's the fault of the manager for picking him. And what is the abuse supposed to achieve? That a player will hear it and suddenly turn into a better player? Yes, we pay our money and can say what we want, but there is a responsibility to back the team, not barrack them. If the player fails, we should ask ourselves 'Was that down to him or did we have a hand in it?' Everyone going out there in blue is representing Rangers, and by extension, us. We have to say, hand on heart, that we gave them the maximum level of encouragement. I'm not sure we can always honestly say that, however. But it is understandable, even if it isn't really acceptable. These guys are out there playing for Rangers, a dream for every supporter that will likely never be realised (I haven't given up hope yet and won't until I'm in a pine box, frankly). If the players fail to show they are worth that spot in the side then they will feel the crowd's wrath. How they handle it is what shapes them. Some, like McCoist and Hateley, have buckled down and won over the doubters. And some have simply shrivelled up and, in occasional cases, their career has never recovered. It's a harsh and unforgiving arena to ply your trade.

There's no getting away from the fact that some of us were a bit spoiled by success. As the memory of those early, pre-Souness days began to dissipate, many people of my generation simply expected to win the League. It was a given; it was what we did. It created a level of success which was probably unsustainable. Also, given the colossal mismanagement at Rangers through the early part of the 21st century, allied to the changes in football worldwide in the wake of the Champions League, the chances of a team from a small country being able to compete in the transfer market are non-existent. Players can earn more money at Bolton than they can at Ibrox. It's a simple and devastating consequence of playing in the Scottish League. You are only as strong as your weakest link, and in Scotland we have a lot of weak links.

This leads into the debate about which team has the greatest fans. Celtic fans have awarded themselves this mantle for reasons that escape anyone who isn't one of them. I'm a great believer that self-praise is no praise; this is not an idea, however, which finds much traction with the other half of Glasgow. I think it came about from Tommy Burns oft-repeated belief that

Celtic fans were, indeed, the 'Greatest Fans in the World'. Apparently, starting to attend matches again after not doing so for a long spell in the early 1990s was the main criteria in this decision. In fairness to Tommy, he was a lifelong Celtic supporter who had played for them and was currently their manager. It is unsurprising he had a somewhat green-tinted view of their followers. But I don't really think we can call Tommy Burns's account an unbiased one, however well-intentioned or heartfelt.

Are Rangers fans, therefore, the 'Greatest Fans in the World' then? No, not in my opinion. You see, if you support Rangers or Celtic, there is a fair old chance you will see your team win more often than they will lose. You will see a lot of silverware in your lifetime, or if you are a Celtic fan my age, some silverware. If you follow Ayr United, or Gillingham, or Bristol Rovers, you probably won't. If you, as a guy I know does, take half-days from work to go see Blackpool play in midweek against Southampton, you have a claim to be the greatest fan in the world. And that, for me, is the issue's core. It's not about a specific support, it's about the individual supporter of any club. If you go to every game and you sing your heart out in good times or bad, you are a great supporter. If you go to as many matches as you can afford, you are a great supporter. If you try to look after your club, to do your best for it, you are a great supporter. I'm a good supporter, not a great one; I see the lengths some of my friends go to to support Rangers and I'm awestruck. It's a level of commitment that exceeds common sense at times. I know guys who managed to get into the game against Inter Milan in the San Siro. Apart from the travel, time off work, hassle from family and other such trifles, there was one fact which made this massively impressive – the game was played behind closed doors. No tickets were issued, and no supporters were allowed in. Yet they managed it. That, my friends, is dedication.

However, I do believe Rangers have, in the main, a terrific support. We've been pilloried, talked down to and abused by the media. We've been shown a callous disregard by the people running the club. Yet still we turn up in our thousands, our away support is utterly fantastic, and we remain the single biggest group of investors in the club through season ticket sales and merchandising. I'm content to know that I'm part of something special.

It's a sign of the Celtic support's manifest insecurity that they don't seem able to just be content with something similar. It's not enough for them to believe they are a great support; they need constant reassurance. It's become a standing joke among the Rangers support. Celtic fans often point out that they received an award from UEFA after their run to Seville in 2003. They don't tend to mention the email campaign to UEFA demanding some recognition that prompted this, however. Similarly, their 'special relationships' with anyone and everyone who they happen to play at some point are laughable. At the last count, Celtic were twinned with Newcastle, Liverpool, Manchester United, Barcelona, AC Milan, Villarreal, Yeovil and Japan. The whole country. Why? Who gives a toss what other teams think of you?

Back to Souness. Many of us felt that when Kenny Dalglish resigned from the Liverpool job in 1990 that Souness would be favourite for the job, and we hoped that he wouldn't be tempted. But it was just too much for him to turn down. From this distance, it's easy to forget just how big the Liverpool job was in 1991. They were the definitive English club. Before Ferguson led Manchester United fully out of the doldrums and into pole position as the undisputed biggest club in England, Liverpool were everybody's second team. Add Souness's time as a player there and it was just too much for him to turn down. What else could he do for Rangers – start a second revolution?

Many people blame Souness for the effect he had on Scottish football as a whole. He brought in too many foreigners, which slowed down the home-grown talent; he encouraged other teams to spend beyond their means to catch up with Rangers; he changed the flavour for Irn Bru, and it's never been the same since. All of this is bollocks, and it's all easily dismissed.

Firstly, the signings from abroad – Souness simply did what other countries had been doing for years. He also brought top-drawer talent from England, which boosted crowds at Ibrox and wherever we played. The argument that the imports stopped young Scottish talent coming through is spurious. I was at school back then – you simply couldn't find teams to play for. Kids of my generation hit a brick wall when they got to their teens. The teachers' strikes of the late 1980s meant that there was little or no extra-curricular activity for children. Many youngsters simply drifted away from the game due to lack of opportunity.

Secondly, he forced other teams to almost bankrupt themselves in a bid to keep up with us. I love this argument, it's so wonderfully loony. Let's just work it through – Rangers are spending money. Therefore, everyone else needs to spend money. But everyone else doesn't have any money. They should spend it anyway. Does anybody else see the problem? If my neighbour buys a big car and I buy one in a fit of jealousy, I can't blame him if the bailiffs come to take it back. The chairmen who overspent have only one person to blame, and they will be able to find him should they look in a mirror. And yes, that goes for David Murray too.

The only thing I have against Souness for leaving is when he chose to do so. He made David Murray aware of his decision with a month of the season left, a season we'd been cantering before a late run of injuries caused us to drop our performances. With a dogged and talented Aberdeen side chasing us – yes, Aberdeen did once have teams capable of that, as opposed to ones that simply provide season-long laughs – we were in a scrap. Souness wanted to hang on until the end of the season, but Murray felt he wouldn't be focused on the job in hand and told him to leave immediately. It was game on, especially after Motherwell hammered us 3–0 at Fir Park to set up a winner-takes-all clash with Aberdeen on the last day of the season.

This seems so anachronistic as to belong to another era, but the game wasn't on the telly. These days it's practically impossible to miss an important match, but back then there were a lot of Bears who had to make do with a radio outside Ibrox. Luckily, we were inside. The tension that day was stomach-churning. You could feel it, see it in people's faces, hear it in their voices. I'd say you could smell it too, but that was probably just the pies.

It was a special day for Rangers fans. Mark Hateley really arrived as a Rangers player that day. With two minutes gone he absolutely flattened the Aberdeen goalkeeper, Michael Watt. These days it would probably lead to a booking, but back then assaulting a goalkeeper was pretty much part of the job spec for a target man. He scored two by half-time, one a glorious header which was a true Hateley trademark (that and scoring braces — he got lots of them, but never a hat-trick). We had the game in the bag, or so you would think.

The problem was that the Rangers team resembled a patchwork quilt. John Brown was playing but could hardly walk. Tom Cowan suffered a leg-break and had to be carried off, and a clearly unfit McCoist had to come off the bench just so we could finish with 11 men. Those two goals had knocked the stuffing out of the Dons, though, and we held on after what seemed like an eternity. The noise that day was incredible, as was the sense of triumph at the end. The fans knew how close we'd come to absolute disaster. Without the steadying influence of the new manager, there's a very good chance nine in a row would have died on its arse that day before it even came close to becoming reality. This momentous victory heralded the era of the new man, the chosen one to replace Souness — Walter Smith.

5

Mr Smith Goes to the Top

It's funny how certain words or phrases enter the lexicon of popular culture from time to time. A few years ago, not many of us knew what a download was. Now your granny does. Similarly, people who entered talent contests used to simply enter talent contests and attempt to win it. Nowadays they go on a 'journey', trying to discover hidden depths through the medium of warbling along to *Don't Stop Believing*. People in pubs were discussing quantative easing, not something I'd have stuck a bet on a few years ago, unless it was a pub frequented by gangs of thirsty economists. Things change.

Football is not exempt from this. One word: metatarsal. Up until David Beckham broke his, most of us were content to simply call a broken foot a broken foot. Post-2002 we all became shop floor doctors, speculating on recovery times and fitness levels. A key word in recent years has been 'stability'. As chairman spent wildly on players in their attempts to 'chase the dream', managers would be sacked and players would be turned over with the frequency of customers in a McDonalds. Someone from the club then preaches the value of stability, stating that a period of prolonged calm will help the club to achieve the level of performance required to reach 'the next level' (there's another one). In practice, this usually leads to another spending splurge on yet more disinterested players, a new manager coming in fighting fires with the urgency of Red Adair on a busy day and the whole process being repeated until the club teeters hopelessly on the brink of financial ruin.

Rangers spoke a lot about stability in 1991 when we appointed Walter Smith as our new manager, only, in our case, we actually did grasp the concept back then. It truly was a different era. Walter had been Souness's first and most important signing. A hugely respected coach, he'd been Jim McLean's assistant at Dundee United and worked with Souness at international level. A Rangers man to the core, Walter had been the number two at Ibrox since the Souness revolution and was thought by many to be the power behind the throne. He'd taken over in the post-departure shitstorm that had engulfed the club and kept calm – and enough players upright – to guide us to the League title. It seemed a no-brainer to appoint him as manager, but it was still a brave move by Murray. Walter wasn't a sexy name, but back then, things like ability counted a bit more than wittering on expansively about ideas you'd picked up from *Coaching for Dummies*.

I don't know if someone like Walter would get the break at a club Rangers size these days. The pressure from the fans to go for what they perceive to be a 'big name' would be enormous. There is often a stigma attached to an assistant taking the reins. The feeling persists that it doesn't offer enough of a sea-change from the previous regime, that what you are doing is simply a continuation of what has gone before. This, to be fair, is a somewhat valid argument in most of the situations when this type of promotion occurs. When England punted Sven Goran Eriksson, for example, they appointed Steve McLaren. There were various reasons for this, of course (the main one being that he was English), but the fact was

Eriksson was leaving because he had been unsuccessful. By bringing in McLaren, they were appointing someone who was tainted by the failure of the previous regime because he had been a huge part of the previous regime. If he knew what was wrong under Eriksson, logic dictated, why didn't he attempt to sort it then?

Smith's ascension was different though. He'd been part of an era of almost unbroken domestic success, the players and media respected him, and the fans were willing to accept the suggestions coming from within Ibrox that he had been a pivotal part of what had gone before. Souness, indeed, had attempted to take him to Liverpool, and his subsequently patchy managerial career would indicate that the Walter factor had been a vital component of his success at Ibrox. From 1991 to the present day, to compare both bosses CVs would lead to a fairly straightforward appraisal: Walter is better.

I was entering a strange period of my life, that adolescent era when you notice those things your female classmates are developing on their chests and can suddenly seem to look at nothing else. I fell in love with girls and music simultaneously, developing long-lasting man crushes on Roger McGuinn, Michael Stipe, Kurt Cobain and Lou Reed. I was the only 14-year-old in Ayrshire who owned Joy Division's *Unknown Pleasures.* I attempted to grow my hair long but discovered that it didn't grow down, only out. I was capable of growing a pretty mean white-man afro, but that was about it. Hence it stayed short. I began reading voraciously about The Beatles, the Rolling Stones and Andy Warhol. I started to read great poetry and write dreadful poetry. I became a right royal pain in the arse around the house, this formerly good boy being now a sort of ginger Pol Pot when asked to perform tasks I considered Herculean, like taking the bins out. I was the living embodiment of Harry Enfield's Kevin the Teenager character. Luckily, so were all my mates.

I remember reading a biography of Led Zeppelin that included tales of what they got up to on the road, including (but not limited to) sticking a fish up a groupie's front bottom, trying to get a Great Dane to have carnal relations with a groupie, hoovering up a fifth of Colombia in powder form and black magic. It is perhaps a touch understandable that I was somewhat more enthused by this than in thinking who'd be in centre-mid for us next season. But it didn't last. Football is like a bug and, once infected, you are a victim for life. You simply can't stop caring. All roads lead back to it, somehow. For me it was the fact that Ibrox remained a place where my dad could take me and I'd behave like an actual human being rather than a monosyllabic farting device. I couldn't normally communicate as freely with grown-ups as I wanted to when I was that age, but I could at the football, because everyone is equal. We were all there to see our team, discuss our them, encourage the players and laugh at Celtic. It's a universal language and even teenagers can speak it.

The three-foreigner rule was in full effect then, whereby teams could only play three players who were not nationals in European competition. This meant the bulk of the team had to be from Scotland, as England was counted as a 'foreign' nation. This seems fair. If we have different national teams, then you can't suddenly claim we are all British when it comes to bypassing a rule everyone else is stuck with. So it was goodbye to Chris Woods and hello to Andy Goram, aka 'the Goalie'. In what must surely rank as one of the finest pieces of transfer business ever conducted by anyone anywhere, ever, Smith sold Woods for £1.2 million and bought in Goram from Hibs for £1 million. Now, Chris Woods was a magnificent goalkeeper for Rangers, but Goram was just something else entirely. He is the finest goalkeeper I have ever seen, and that is not an exaggeration. Many great players have played for Rangers in my lifetime. Some were world-class. But Goram was simply in a class of his own. He made the unbelievable routine. He could save efforts that he had no right to be in the same postcode as. You just couldn't stop him from being brilliant. And what's more, he really did connect with the fans as he looked like one of us, down to the pot belly and the bleary eyes. Andy really did embrace the Ibrox culture, perhaps a little too much at times. One remembers his black armband in the week Loyalist paramilitary Billy Wright was killed. Andy claimed it was, in fact, a tribute to his Auntie Lil, who had died some six weeks before. Maybe it was a matter of timing, but it certainly looked a bit suspect.

In my lifetime it has been noticeable that Rangers have always been blessed with great 'keepers, while our rivals have tended to be landed with, let's be polite here, shite ones. When you have a line that is basically Woods, Goram, Klos, Wattereus and McGregor, you are witnessing something very special. In that time, Celtic's desperation to find a goalkeeper who was the equal of those across the city became ever more acute. It included such household names as Ian Andrews, Carl Muggleton and Jonathan Gould. Whenever a young Celtic goalie emerged who looked as though he could occasionally be trusted to gather the ball without chucking it in, he was lauded as 'the saviour'. Stewart Kerr was supposed to go on to rival Ronnie Simpson; it didn't happen. David Marshall was, however, the best example. He came in as an unheralded youngster for a match against Barcelona in the UEFA Cup, and he was superb. It was an outstanding performance, but the landslide that followed ended up crushing him. The papers went completely bonkers for him, to the point that by the week's end people had been subjected to a feature on him walking his dog. That was front-page news. Never ones to give a youngster time, the boy was placed under pressure to be the Scottish Iker Cassillas, which was too much for him. He'd had the game of his life that night and was never able to replicate that form consistently because he simply wasn't that good. The final manifestation of this came in Artur Boruc. If ever a guy was born to play for Celtic, it was Artur. He was a professional athlete but the size of a Jeremy Kyle guest, and talented, but nowhere near as good as they needed him to be. The Celtic FC correspondents in the Scottish press, led by Peter Lawell's chief slave Mark Guidi, described him as 'the best in the world,' and he was forever being 'looked at' by Europe's biggest football clubs for fees of up to £14 million. Except, of course, he wasn't. The bids never materialised due to the fact that Artur was somewhat let down by an IQ in single digits and the unerring gift for throwing one in every third big game. As for his antics, they simply underlined why no Polish comedian has ever sold out the Carnegie Hall.

Goram wasn't the only Scot. With players like John Brown, Davie Robertson, Dave McPherson, Stuart McCall, Richard Gough and Ally McCoist, we had an unmistakeably Scottish core and identity. This was important, not only from a European point of view, but also for giving us a healthy, 'home' feel. We blasted off into that season and just looked comfortable from the off. A Goram mistake cost us the League Cup semi against Hibs, but after that no one could touch us. We played a fluid 4–4–2, leading to McCoist and Hateley, who were deadly. If teams wanted a scrap, we could scrap. There was no point 'getting in our faces', in the style of Arsenal, because we were just as likely to boot you in the George Dawes and take the ball as we were to pass you off the park. There was real fire in the bellies of the guys in blue that season. We were a joy to watch.

We ended our miserable Scottish Cup record that season too. While the League Cup had always been good to us during the 1980s, the Scottish Cup had seemed to exist solely to remind us that we were human. Apart from the Hamilton defeat, we had also crashed out to Dunfermline, a side who simply didn't beat us normally – our very presence was usually enough to see them off. Celtic definitely had our measure in the Cup, no matter what was happening in the League. We lost twice in the early rounds to them, including a game that was mental, even by Old Firm standards, and we ended up with eight players. Then there was the 1989 Scottish Cup Final, which Celtic won 1–0 to deny us a treble. The winning goal was scored by Joe Miller, a winger who was a cross between a footballer and ET. He looked like that anyway. The goal remains one of the most controversial in Old Firm history. The ball went out for what was clearly a Rangers throw. Roy Aitken, the Celtic player, got up and took the throw in. The referee seemed to be operating by the lesser-known 'whoever gets to the ball first can take the throw-in' rule and did not call the ball back.

It ended with a slack backpass from Gary Stevens being turned in by Miller. This illustrates a key difference between the two supports; had this gone the other way, we'd never have heard the end of it. Rangers fans, while a bit miffed at the cheating, curly-haired bastard, understood that things like that happen in football. Anyway, Stevens should have dealt with the backpass.

If ever a match summed up a football team, it was the Scottish Cup semi-final that season. It was an Old Firm match and had drama from the opening minutes. It was an absolutely filthy night at the old Hampden, which wasn't the most comfortable of venues at the best of times. The rain was teeming down, black sheets of water drenching anyone unfortunate enough to get caught up in it. It certainly didn't cool things down on the field, however. After just five minutes Davie Robertson was sent off for bringing down Joe Miller. It was a ludicrous decision, Miller going down as if pole-axed after an innocuous hold-off from the full-back. Terry Butcher was providing commentary on a nascent Sky channel, and he certainly seemed to be outraged by the decision. He suggested that Miller had deliberately made the foul look worse and was 'walking around pleased with himself that he's got a fellow pro sent-off'. These days, it's part of the game for players to do that, but back then it really seemed to stick in Terry's throat. After that, a Rangers player would have needed to bring out an open razor and attack a Celtic player with it before Terry would have felt it was a foul, never mind a booking. It was game over after just five minutes. We were out, and it was pissing with rain, and the Celtic fans were singing. We were not in a good place.

Celtic battered us, with Paul McStay particularly impressive in midfield. Confession time: I always liked him as a player and admired him as a man. He was Celtic through and through, but he carried himself with an air of class. That night, his passing was in full flow, and we couldn't get the ball off him. But this was the night Andy Goram was to start what would, at times over the next five years, look like a one-man campaign to prevent Celtic scoring. He was flinging himself left and right, catching and turning away everything that was thrown at him. And it was a lot. Celtic went into full-on 'charge' mode, and at times it looked like if they could just get one goal, they could run up a cricket score.

This is where football is at its very best. The tension in the air and the knowledge that if they got one, we were highly unlikely to be able to reply, lent every attack a frisson of real danger. Equally, every attack that broke down, every move that petered out or ended in another brilliant save increased the frustration at the other end of the ground. You could feel it rising from the Celtic support. It began to transmit to the team and we started to get a foothold in the game, without, it must be said, looking like we were going to score. And then, out of nowhere, Stuart McCall broke with the ball just before half-time and slipped a pass through to Ally McCoist, who dispatched a shot into the bottom corner. The Rangers end just erupted – it was a primal, intense explosion of unbridled joy and no small relief. Ally's celebration was sheer, raw emotion; he slid on his knees and seemed to cry, though that could just have been the rain. The second half saw Celtic hit the bar and Goram continue to defy them with exceptional shot-stopping, but the sense enveloped the ground that this was our night. They knew it, and we knew it. They were well beaten before the final whistle went.

This meant the Final against Airdrie couldn't compare, and it didn't really. We won 2–1 without playing well, and fittingly McCoist and Hateley got the two goals. We had won the double, the first time I had witnessed us doing so. Just to see us carry the famous old trophy around – for the first time since 1981 – made the day special, even if the Final hadn't been particularly easy on the eye. It was a great time to be a supporter. We had ambition, and we seemed to have big plans in place. We were comfortably the best team in the country and we were about to embark on what we felt could be a serious crack at the European Cup. No one could tell just how serious it would turn out to be.

6

Glory Days

When criticising David Murray (as I seem to have spent a lot of my time in the noughties doing in my role as spokesman for the largest independent supporters' group, the Rangers Supporters' Trust) it was often important to remember that, for all his failings in his second decade as chairman, in his early days he presided over a club where the sun always seemed to be shining. He was dynamic in a way other chairmen just weren't; he was probably the first of the generation of owners who became as integral to the day-to-day visibility of the club as the manager. He was everywhere in the media, who absolutely lapped him up. He upgraded the capacity of Ibrox by building another level on the Main Stand. He was always willing to put his money where his mouth was in terms of signings. He seemed ambitious but, more importantly, possessed with an innate desire to deliver what he said he would. Rangers in 1992 were, undoubtedly, one of the biggest clubs in Europe. Apart from the historical continental superpowers, we seemed able to compete with anybody. Manchester United hadn't secured that elusive League title yet. Liverpool were in the midst of the decline which, domestically, hasn't really arrested itself at the time of writing. Arsenal were a very good side but not one who gave you nightmares. Berlusconi's AC Milan had proven to be the best team in Europe over the previous few seasons, with Barcelona under the management of Johan Cruyff the next best, beating Sampdoria at Wembley in 1992 to win the inaugural Champions League. Those two sides apart, however, it was all up for grabs. The English were just catching up with Scotland by launching their own Premiership, something we'd had since 1975 (immediately, though, theirs became the definitive, with ours being fitted with a prefix 'Scottish' so we would know our place). No one could quite see how the shake-up European football was undergoing would pan out, but it was an exciting time and if we weren't quite at the forefront, we'd definitely got a seat on the plane. It made you feel like pretty much anything was possible.

There was an inescapable feeling of possibility in the early 1990s. As a country, everything in Scotland just seemed a bit brighter. The 1980s had seemed to last forever, and while nostalgia shows today try to suggest it was all Audi Quattros and New Romantics, that wasn't really Scotland. Thatcher, the biggest political bogeyman ever, had been deposed – I use the term pointedly – in 1990. The Poll Tax riots were a thing of the past, with large swathes of the country settling into contented non-payment strategies. Scotland seemed liberated, almost optimistic. This is not a feeling we Scots naturally have. Think about it – what is the default response of a happy Scot when you ask them how they are doing? 'I'm not bad.' In other words, 'I don't feel particularly wonderful, but nothing unspeakably awful has happened to me today, so I suppose I should be grateful for that and get on with it.' I blame the rain.

Our biggest challenge seemed set to come from what, in hindsight, was the last great Aberdeen team. Celtic were withering under the disastrous ownership of the family dynasties that had ruled over them like incompetent Tsars for decades. Their latest saviour was Dr Michael Kelly, a former Lord Provost, whose greatest claim to fame was that he had come up with the 'Glasgow's Miles Better' advertising campaign. This piece of epic whimsy was, to most people, not a massively impressive CV entry for the post of running a gigantic football club, or even Celtic, but that and the fact his second name was 'Kelly' seemed to be enough for him to get the job. The hooped hordes seemed happy. One caller to Radio Clyde's phone-in show unforgettably suggested that 'signing Dr Kelly off the park is like signing Maradona on it'. I miss Dr Mike, with his wispy beard adorning his hangdog jowls. He always reminded me of Droopy, the cartoon dog. It was a sad day when Celtic stopped hiring people like him to run their affairs and instead started hiring people who were mostly competent. We went the other way, of course.

Aberdeen had a really good side under the management of Pittodrie legend Willie Miller, another good moustache wearer. There wasn't, and isn't, much love lost between our two sides, though as a kid I remember that Celtic and Aberdeen seemed to have a mutual loathing of each other, more so than any massive rivalry we had with Aberdeen. Perhaps that was because they were going for League titles, while we were generally out of the running by March. For example, Gordon Strachan was once famously assaulted on the pitch at Parkhead during a particularly heated fixture when he was starring for Aberdeen. But when Souness arrived, Aberdeen's status as Scottish football top dogs was over almost as quickly as it had begun. They didn't take kindly to that, and fixtures between the two sides were always combustible.

The incident that truly heralded the game as a real hatefest occurred in October 1988, when Ian Durrant, Rangers' gifted young midfielder, was left with his knee destroyed by a tackle from Aberdeen midfielder Neil Simpson. I say 'tackle', but 'murderous lunge' would probably be more fitting. Durrant's knee buckled, and he was out for almost three years. Although he returned and had a very decent career with Rangers and Kilmarnock, he was never quite the same player. Souness had said he felt Durrant was destined to go to the very top, possibly even Serie A. Simpson had stamped down over the ball, a moment where he had lost control of his senses. There is no doubt that the tackle was intended to hurt Durrant – how could it not be? When you stamp down on someone's knee while nowhere near the ball, what else are you trying to? Watch the footage – the light of sanity has gone from his eyes and there's a hollow blackness there. We speak a lot in football about intent. If Simpson really didn't intend to hurt Durrant, then why make that tackle?

I've heard idiots say that two careers were ended that day. Simpson's career also effectively finished then because he never really recovered from the stigma, but that's just bullshit that paints the perpetrator of the crime as the victim. Did Simpson need to have his knee surgically rebuilt? Does his knee bear the scars of those countless operations? Was he on crutches for nearly a year? No. So why should anyone feel sorry for him? He went out to injure a fellow pro, and he did. Why is he not regarded with the same contempt as Ioan Ganea, the Romanian thug who did the same to John Kennedy, the promising Celtic centre-half?

This incident really did speed up the move from this being a football rivalry to a more personal thing between the clubs. Aberdeen fans immediately started to glorify it by singing sick songs about Durrant lying injured on the turf, his career over. They still do this, almost a quarter of a century later. For me and other Rangers fans, it simply puts the final seal on the notion that Aberdeen are at heart a small-time club who got lucky for a few years under a phenomenal manager. Injuring an opposition player is their claim to fame. If that's the thing you clutch closest to your heart, then you've got problems. Aberdeen fans claim to dislike Rangers (and the West Coast of Scotland as a whole) because we're hate-filled bigots. They should certainly know. I've never seen anything more hate-filled than the Aberdeen support when we play them.

Going to Pittodrie just isn't a pleasant experience. Not in a Galatasaray 'welcome to hell' way, more an 'I hope I don't have to touch anything in this place and get home without contracting rabies' kind of fashion. Undeniably, this stems from one inescapable fact – it's an absolute shithole. If stadiums were television programmes, this would be *EastEnders* – it used to be good, but now it's just so old and irrelevant that when you see it, it almost makes you cry with embarrassment. Aberdeen's fanbase has also drifted away over the years. Actually, most Scottish clubs have seen their support decrease steadily since the 1980s, with the exception of Rangers and, to be fair, Celtic. Yet Old Firm fans are routinely labelled 'glory-hunters'. In 2010, however, St Mirren and Dundee United got to the League and Scottish Cup Finals respectively, and they sold far more tickets than their average home gate. So where are these diehards every other week? I don't have a problem with the community attending big games, incidentally, it just annoys me when supporters who attend week-in, week-out are labelled 'glory-hunters' by people who don't actually go every week. It's widescale hypocrisy.

Aberdeen's falling support levels means their stadium is hardly ever full any more, and it isn't that big to begin with. There is no obvious reason for this, Aberdeen being a prosperous, one-club city, apart from the argument suggesting that their support simply got fed up watching the dross they have served up from the mid-90s onwards. The fans who have remained have tried to remain stoic and defiant in the face of the ever-enveloping sense of faded glory that hangs around the club like a haar coming in from the North Sea. They've also tried to develop a sense of identity, which has seen them try on different personas in the manner of a teenage girl trying to find herself. For a while they positioned themselves as 1980s throwback casuals, being violent whilst dressed in Pringle jumpers. It was like being attacked by a tribe of unintelligible golfers. They then tried to grab smug underdog authority, the poor wee team who stood up to the horrible big Glasgow club. This failed entirely as they also saw themselves as better than the rest of the Scottish League, and it's extremely difficult to be a champion of the little people while simultaneously looking down your nose at them. Then they decided they would be the Roy 'Chubby' Brown of Scottish Football, the amusing ones who were shocking and outrageous. They were neither, but they were unpleasant and exceptionally irritating. They call themselves the 'Red Army'. Given their sporadic appearances, they should more accurately be called the 'Red TA'. Their away support call themselves the 'Red Ultras' in a nod to Italian fan culture, which tries to position themselves as more extreme and somewhat more dangerous than the average fan. And best of all, they try to claim a massive rivalry with Rangers.

They really hate us, but it's pretty one-sided. I guarantee you the first result an Aberdeen fan looks for after their own is the Rangers score. It would never occur to me to look up the Aberdeen score, unless they were playing Celtic, in which case I would want them to win. This is not the sign of a bitter rivalry. It's the equivalent of Burnley telling Manchester United fans that they are their biggest enemies. Dream on. They chased away a successful manager, Jimmy Calderwood, because he was a Glaswegian with Rangers sympathies, and they replaced him with Mark McGhee, who made a right royal arse of it. Well done, guys!

This 'rivalry' has led to some surreal sights. A goal for Aberdeen against us is greeted with the demented joy of a teenage boy getting his hand round a young lady's funbags for the first time. You would think they'd won the World Cup. Meanwhile, our goals against them – which are, admittedly, far more regular – are greeted with the same joy of our goals against Falkirk or St Mirren, other perennial bottom-six clubs. There's no point getting excited, it's just Aberdeen. After a while their shock-jock tactics, with songs about Durrant, the death of Davie Cooper or the Ibrox Disaster, just sound like what they are – the pathetic death rattle of a club whose supporters aren't so much attention-seeking as attention-hostage taking, so desperate are they for attention of any sort that they'd probably set fire to their own arses if they thought it would get them on Sky Sports News. The sad truth is that they just do not count. They are an annoyance, but only in the way a buzzing wasp is an annoyance at a picnic. You swat them away every so often and they give you peace. This is the relationship between Rangers fans and Aberdeen fans. They do not count. They do not matter. For us, it's like getting wound up about Third Lanark.

You can only beat what's put in front of you, as the cliché goes. Rangers certainly did that in 1992–93, at one point going an incredible 44 games without defeat. The most impressive thing about this run was that it really was a team effort. While we had obvious leaders, such as Goram, Gough, McCall, Ferguson, Hateley and McCoist, this was not a side of splintered individualism or one exceptional player who lifted a good side into the realms of greatness. Everyone had a part to play and knew what they were supposed to do. There was also a sense of togetherness from players and fans that helped propel us further than most would have felt possible.

We won the League Cup after beating Aberdeen 2–1 at Hampden with the help of the new-fangled passback rule. Aberdeen defender Gary Smith knocked the ball back towards his own goal. 'Keeper Theo Snelders wasn't sure if he could handle it or not so he chested it away rather comedically, and Stuart McCall scored to equalise. This is a good representation of what happens every time FIFA introduces a major new rule into the sport. Spectators and fans are often understandably unsure of the grey areas, which FIFA usually hilariously compound by giving referees about 18 different 'interpretations' of it, thus meaning that high comedy ensues as spectators see different decisions for about three years until it all settles down. Credit where it's due, it does increase drama. Smith then compounded his memorable day by heading in a Houchenesque beauty of an own-goal in injury time to win the Cup for us.

In late 1992, however, only one thing was on the mind of British football fans, at least according to the sections of the press who like overexaggerations as much as they like clichés (although I must admit I do quite like those). The game which was, more accurately, causing a fair amount of interest in the UK was the Battle of Britain: the Champions League qualifier between Rangers and the English Champions, Leeds United. This was massive in so many ways, chief of which was the rekindling of the rivalry between Scotland and England at the national game. The annual match between the two home nations had ended in 1989 after a rather turgid 2–0 win for the English. It was a shame because it was definitely a day on the calendar to look forward to. The widening sphere of nutters who attached themselves to the England team did cause the authorities to have a think about whether or not it was all worth it. In the end they concluded that it wasn't, and who can blame them? It was a match that caused them headaches and didn't really have much of a reason to exist apart from national pride. Having to plan and pay for the containment of lagered-up loonies with skinheads and bad intentions probably wasn't their idea of well-deployed resources.

Leeds had won the last-ever First Division title in England and were stylistically a traditionally British side, much like ourselves. They had a strong Scottish identity, with Gordon Strachan and Rangers fan Gary McAllister making up the central midfield (McAllister almost signed for us in 1995, but Leeds refused the offer and we signed Paul Gascoigne instead). Up front they had Lee Chapman as their target man, performing the Hateley role. Next to him was a chap who was, at the time, simply regarded as an exceptional, if slightly eccentric, footballer, Eric Cantona. His best days were yet to come, and he'd become one of *the* figures of the early Premiership for his goals, his attitude and his quite magnificent karate kick on a fan at Selhurst Park. I know it was terrible, but how cool was it? 99.9 per cent of people wouldn't have even contemplated kicking the bloke. Punch, yes, but kick? Magnificent! Football fans have grown into little girls about things like this. Granted, you shouldn't get kicked in the chest, but it really annoys me when fans give out 90 minutes of exceptionally vile abuse and then faint like maiden aunts seeing a willy when a footballer gestures back. If you can give it out, learn to take it.

The anticipation for the match was just gigantic. The English press thought, for some reason, that it was effectively a bye for Leeds. It was a qualifier for the new-fangled Champions League, the first time a British club would participate in it, following a ban on English clubs taking part in European competitions after the Heysel disaster. It's almost unimaginable to modern minds, though — can anyone truly visualise UEFA telling Manchester United or Chelsea that they weren't going to be able to participate in the Champions League? Leeds route had been a controversial one; in their match with German champions Stuttgart they had been beaten over the two legs only to find that the German club had used four foreign players in the second leg. How the Stuttgart manager didn't notice that is one for the ages. UEFA, who hated the English League even then, before Platini made it obvious, ordered a one-match decider at the neutral Nou Camp. There was absolutely no chance they'd have done that if it had been Leeds who had fielded an ineligible player. Leeds duly triumphed, and the hype machine, such as it was, started to whirr. I say that because there was no Sky Sports News back then and no internet, so the game was just a very attractive fixture on the card. The first leg wasn't even live on the telly up here, being shown on delayed transmission after the match had ended.

The authorities decided that away fans would not be permitted to attend either leg, which created an odd, if electric atmosphere at Ibrox. The noise was thunderous, a real fever pitch. For 90 seconds, when Gary McAllister thundered in an absolute rocket on the volley from 20 yards, there was nothing. There is nothing more eerie in a stadium than dead silence, and that was what greeted the goal. You could hear the Leeds bench celebrating, followed by a chorus of muttered 'f**ksakes' until the defiant roar of the crowd returned.

We got back on level terms with a real poacher's goal from McCoist and then battered them. However, we only scored one more, and what a truly bizarre goal it was. Leeds 'keeper John Lukic came for a corner then seemed to forget what he was doing. Maybe he noticed a friend in the crowd, but when he suddenly remembered just why he was in the middle of the six-yard box he made an awkward attempt at punching the ball and only succeeded in deflecting it into his own net. He later tried to blame the floodlights, saying he'd lost the flight of the ball in the light. This does beg the question why he never conceded another goal like that in his career when playing midweek games. It ended 2–1, with Leeds fancying their chances due to the away goal. It did, in truth, look like we had a tall order ahead of us.

The second leg was preceded with dire warnings of consequences for travelling fans trying to sneak into the home crowd. Many did though, with slightly hilarious consequences, as the game started in the same way, a magnificent early opener after 90 seconds. Only this time, it was

Rangers, when Hateley turned his foot round a ball on the drop and it absolutely exploded into the top corner. It was an incredible strike, and it seemed to inspire the rest of his team. The Rangers fans who had gained entry leapt up instinctively to cheer it, and were summarily chucked out. It was one of those goals, though; it seemed to come from nothing, you were celebrating before you realised what you were doing. It was an almost primal reaction. Leeds battered us, but Andy Goram was having one of his 'nae danger are you bastards scoring' games. He was unbelievable. Everything they threw at us, he mopped up imperiously. Cantona, in particular, seemed to have annoyed him as Andy waged a one-man war against the Frenchman.

In the second half, with Leeds really on top, we launched one of the best counter-attacking moves I have ever seen, with several one-twos up the park resulting in Hateley finding his strike partner with a sublime curling cross and Ally bulleting a diving header back across the goalkeeper and into the far corner. Leeds now needed four, and, frankly, they weren't getting them. Ally's unbridled joy was in wonderful contrast to the faces of the Leeds players, who knew that they were going out. They got one back, as Cantona finally proved the law of averages is a sound one by getting on the scoresheet, but it didn't matter. We were through. We were the first British team in the Champions League. Rangers rubbed salt in the wounds of the English media by releasing a video of the whole tie that featured the English commentary. Listening to the tag-team of the venerable Brian Moore and the extraordinary musings of Ron Atkinson was well worth the price. Atkinson was a truly special commentator. He developed his own, unique commentary style that consisted of strange phrases like 'up go the eyebrows' or 'back stick'. One needed a degree in Ronglish to get through the 90 minutes with him. His simmering disbelief at what he was watching in the second leg was hilarious to behold.

The draw pitted us with Marseilles, Bruges and CSKA Moscow. Only eight teams made it into two groups of four back then, with the winners of each meeting in the Final. This was back when UEFA operated under the crazy system of only allowing the Champions of each League into the Champions League. It added a real topping of glamour to an otherwise routine League season as we swatted aside every team who faced us. We were flying, and the big games seemed to come thick and fast. Celtic were just woeful at this point in their history, under the dynamic leadership of Liam Brady, who'd been appointed for reasons that were never actually explained. He was Irish, so I suppose that helped, and had been really good at football, but past that it was a struggle to see why he was the one out of the dozens of names linked who would be able to restore Celtic to the pinnacle of Scottish football. He seemed a nice man, although always a little confused at the limitless maelstrom that seemed to engulf him. He was the first Celtic manager I remember feeling a bit sorry for, though, thankfully for my laughter lines, not the last.

Aberdeen remained a challenge, though, which was good for us. You need competition to keep you sharp. That said, our minds were firmly focused on Europe. It just seemed so desperately glamorous, like being offered foie gras after a steady diet of pies. The first game came amidst mounting excitement and saw the visit of Marseilles, who were packed full of top-quality players. In goal they had the enigmatic Fabien Barthez. They had Abedi Pele, a talented African whose sheer chutzpah I admired; if you are going to be a footballer, going under the moniker of the biggest icon in the history of the sport demonstrates an admirable level of self-belief. It's like going into boxing and calling yourself Muhammad Ali. They had Alen Boksic up front, a hugely impressive striker whose languid style masked some serious ability. And they had Rudi Voller, the poodle-permed German who is still remembered for being spat on by Frank Rijkaard at Euro '88 and resembling Gnasher from *The Beano*. He could play, though, and was one of the greatest strikers of his generation. They had been funded by the French sportswear magnate Bernard Tapie, who seemed like a Continental version of David Murray. It would all end in tears for him, however.

Ibrox was packed and wet on the night of the game. My memory of the opening 80 minutes is a bit hazy. I remember the opposition being really, really good at football. They played in little triangles but could switch to a more direct style when it suited them and they were quick. Racehorse quick. You knew instantly that this was a step-up in class. They went 2–0 up and, in truth, we could have no real complaints. But the character in Smith's side was to be demonstrated by a comeback that can only be described as 'stirring' (I said I quite liked tabloid clichés). One of the consequences of the three foreigners rule was that the bench often featured young Scottish players. One of those players, Gary McSwegan, came off the bench to cement his place in Rangers folklore with a strangely beautiful goal. He found himself unmarked in the box and sent a header towards the top of the Copland Road Stand. However, after initially looking like it could be Scotland's first item in space, the ball started dropping and curling and ended up slamming into the top corner of Barthez's goal. It seemed to take about three days to go in, and Ibrox was frozen in place as everyone – players, fans, the media, officials – stood back and watched its progress. When it went in, the place exploded into a bone-shuddering, brain-scouring cauldron of noise. The term 'cheers' doesn't really cover it. It was a noise which had been near the throat of every fan since kick-off, lingering hopefully, and the relief at being able to let it go propelled the sound levels up 15 decibels. The old place was shaking. We had a few minutes left to try to get the equaliser. When it came, it came from the old warhorse Hateley. Cue complete meltdown in the stands. I've never known Ibrox to celebrate a draw like that. The noise was almost indescribable, like nothing I'd heard before. Imagine Iron Maiden playing in your living room through a megaphone, and you still won't be close.

We certainly left an impression on the opposition. Barthez later recalled that 'we were thrown to a veritable wild horde. It was a meeting of warriors where neither weakness nor nonchalance had a place.' I'll give the French their due, they certainly know how to make the phrase 'it was really loud' sound exotic. He added, 'It was a test in pure British tradition.' The atmosphere that night was something special.

One of the myths peddled in the media up here is that Parkhead, or the newly built Meccano version created by Fergus McCann out of lollipop sticks and concrete, somehow has a magical aura Ibrox can't measure up to. This is blatant nonsense, but it seems to keep the 'Greatest Fans in the World' happy. This is not to suggest that Parkhead isn't impressive when it is in full voice. There is no doubt in my mind that some of their exceptional European results in the last decade have been fuelled by the passionate support of their home crowd. It's simply the impression that certain commentators like to give that Parkhead is some sort of modern cathedral compared to Ibrox, which contains a few thousand punters flicking through a paper while occasionally casting their eyes towards the field to keep up to date with the match. Ibrox in full voice is an absolute den where you can feel the history soaking through from the walls and into the fans, like a battery being recharged. Don't believe me though, believe Fabien.

Next up was a creditable draw with Bruges in Belgium before we took on CSKA Moscow in neutral Germany. Ian Ferguson got the only goal there, and the bandwagon was well and truly rolling. We really seemed capable of winning the whole bloody thing. The European Cup, that millstone around our collective necks, which the Celtic fan had always had over us.

Next up was the home leg against Bruges. This game will forever be remembered for Scott Nisbet's goal. Big Nizzy was the dictionary definition of 'cult hero'. He wasn't the most mobile or the quickest, never really had an eye for a pass, wasn't particularly good with the ball at his feet and you'd never say he was great in the air. These minor quibbles aside, he was game for anything, playing just about every outfield position for Rangers, and you could never doubt his commitment or energy. The goal that he will be forever remembered for was uncharitably called a fluke by all of those who saw it, but still! With the match level, Mark Hateley had been sent off for an off-the-ball clash with a Bruges defender, who went down far too easily, and we were starting to get pinned back by the Belgian side. At this moment Nisbet, playing at full-back, went in for a challenge and blasted the ball off his opponent's shins. The ball looped up at a crazy angle and at some considerable speed. This took the goalkeeper by surprise, as he'd wandered out into no man's land and was somewhat alarmed to see the ball going over his head, into the turf and then spinning into the net. Nisbet's celebration was one of the most joyous things I have ever seen as he deliriously ran around Ibrox in stunned jubilation. It was starting to look like our year.

The one nagging worry when we left Ibrox that night was that Hateley's sending-off and subsequent suspension may prove costly for us. The big man was absolutely pivotal to us and had been terrorising defences all over the continent. This would prove to be justified when we made our way to the velodrome in Marseilles to play the next match. I wanted to go, but my Dad wasn't up for it and, being 15, it was tough to win the argument. I did offer up one almighty strop about it, though it was to no avail. I was similarly heartbroken when my dad wouldn't let his mate from work take me to see Warren Zevon in concert in London that year. Although my Dad trusted him implicitly, my Mum couldn't quite bring herself to allow her teenage boy to travel with an unmarried man in his forties for unspoken Glitter-related reasons.

We lost a goal to an excellent Franck Sauzée strike. I'd have given you long odds on him becoming a Hibs legend as the ball struck our net, but football is a funny old game, as someone once said. Ian Durrant got our equaliser with a terrific goal, and we ended with a creditable draw, which meant we needed to win our last match and hope Marseilles didn't win theirs to progress. Many have suggested we'd have won that night with Hateley available, but that way madness lies. He wasn't available, we didn't win, end of story.

So to the last match, against CSKA Moscow, who'd been the disappointment of the group. We absolutely battered them, a Sonny on Carlo in the Godfather type kicking, but, like Sonny, we just didn't complete the job. We couldn't score. No matter what happened, we could not get the bloody thing into their net. We really couldn't have done much more, but it was one of those nights. At the end, the mood was desolate. Players wept. Fans wept too, though they were quickly told by their friends to buck up and act like a man.

Crying at the football was rare back then, but it has become an ever-more-common sight. I've never felt like crying at a football match, certainly not in disappointment. It's a football match, for God's sake. I know we all take it too seriously – this is not me having a massive deficit of self-understanding – but is your life really that bad that defeat in a football match tips you over the edge? Get out more. Have a Coke and a smile and shut the f**k up, as Richard Pryor put it. Sky are the masters of finding some deluded arsewit bawling his eyes out after a defeat. It's hard to feel anything other than contempt for people who do it. Get up, get your mates and dissect the game in peace.

Marseilles won the Champions League that year by defeating AC Milan 1–0 in the Final, thanks to a goal from Basile Boli. The match was dire, memorable only for Boli's dreadful challenge on Marco van Basten, which effectively ended the great Dutchman's career. Indeed, it was this tackle which brought about the outlawing of the tackle from behind quicker than expected. We could take comfort from the fact that we had been knocked out by the eventual winners. After all, you can't fight fate.

Marseilles were later stripped of their French title (though not their European Cup) after being found guilty of match-fixing. They had bribed opponents in the French League to ensure victory in certain matches. While there was no evidence they'd done the same in European competition, it still smelled as fishy as a dead fish left out in the sun. That said, I don't think many Rangers fans feel they were cheated out of the trophy. For a start we'd still have had to have beaten a Milan side widely and correctly considered the finest in Europe at the time. Secondly, we gave everything against Marseilles. They were a very decent side. It wasn't their players' fault that their owner was bent. We simply fell a wee bit short.

There was no disgrace in that, and we were the envy of all the other big British clubs as we swanned about Europe in the premier competition. We've been in the Champions League many times since, but it has never been as sweet. Part of that is due to our performances – we've often been almost perversely rubbish, like we've gone out of our way to be a whole other level of mince. But that's not the only reason. The Champions League has since been diluted, poked, prodded and homogenised into the Frankenstein's monster we see now. It isn't about competition, it is purely and simply about money. And this money is very specifically earmarked for the biggest clubs to take, spend and then repeat the process again. The Champions League has lost the innocence it had when it originally appeared. This is, I suppose, an inevitable development, but it doesn't mean you can't mourn for what it was.

The factor that made the early Champions League so special was that all the teams entering felt they had a realistic chance, no matter how small, of winning. When the draw was made, fans could get excited and allow their minds to dream of lifting the famous old trophy. That seems laughably quaint now. The Champions League isn't designed for that any more. Witness the strange situation of Inter Milan, one of Europe's richest and most historically successful clubs. When they finally won it, it was a bit of a shock. Commentators proclaimed how positive it was for football that someone different had added their name to the honour roll. And this was Inter Milan! If they are looked upon as gatecrashers to the top table, what are the chances for the rest of us? For Rangers, our ambitions have had to resize over the years. At first it was the ultimate dream of the support that one day we would win it. Then it became getting out of the group stages. Now it has become getting into the group stages. These days the Champions League, for the SME football clubs, has become a financial event first and foremost. It's as if Michel Platini has donned a top hat and stands handing out golden tickets to European clubs, with most of the clubs entering cast as Charlie Bucket, just delighted to be at the party. But we know our role. We are there to give the top clubs someone to play, to allow the TV people to have a group section before the important matches start to happen in the knock-out stages. BATE Borisov? Unirea Urziceni? Rangers? Schalke 04? Not interested. It all exists to keep the event going until the 865th match between Liverpool and Chelsea, before Barcelona play Manchester United. A core of around eight clubs are the meat of the event, the rest of us range from potatoes to side salad. It's not right, and it's not all that interesting, but that's what it is.

We ended that season with a fifth League title in a row and the chance to win a domestic treble against an Aberdeen side desperate to avoid finishing treble runners-up. Intriguingly, this match was to be played at Parkhead because Hampden was being redeveloped. That meant we had the chance to win the treble in the Jungle. Domestic trebles are, of course, the definitive 'we are the best' statement. It means that no one has been good enough to stop you from completing a clean sweep, that you haven't been vulnerable enough to even let one of the less important trophies slip away. It gives the support the right to affect an almost regal air, as if you are above frippery such as football debate. You simply spend your summer swanning around your workplace smiling benignly at those less-fortunate followers of other sides, exuding a smug and thoroughly deserved confidence, which is borne of sweet, sweet triumph. It's fun. And when you get to do it against one team you can't stand, in the home of another, it's enough to make even the most jaded fan feel that tell-tale tingle. We beat Aberdeen 2–I that day, the first goal coming from a most unlikely source in young midfielder Neil Murray. When we reminisce about days gone by it's easy to remember the McCoists, Hateleys and Goughs and forget about the less-celebrated players. Then you remember people like Neil Murray and marvel at how he ever got a game for us. Young Neil was a thoroughly decent chap, but he looked like an accountant and, sadly, he played like one. He didn't appear to be good at anything, more an amalgam of averageness whom Walter could rely to perform averagely in a variety of positions. All that said, he's scored a goal for Rangers in a Cup Final and I haven't – yet – so who's laughing at whom?

We did it without Ally, who had broken his leg while on Scotland duty. Scotland had failed to qualify for the 1994 World Cup in America, the low point of a fairly awful campaign coming in a 5–0 humping from Portugal in which, legend has it, Scotland had been sent out with instructions devised from information Craig Brown had received from a Portuguese taxi-driver. Having witnessed the display that night, my lasting memory of the match is that we'd have been better playing the taxi-driver, such was the lack of passion from the Scotland team. My patriotism has waned as I have grown older, as has my interest in the national side. I was still a committed fan at that point, but I recall this being the first night I realised I cared more about club than country. My immediate reaction as Ally lay there prone – Ally didn't exaggerate injury, ever; if he was lying down, it was because he was seriously hurt – was that he'd be missing for Rangers and I was bloody raging. Of course, Ally was the poster boy of Ibrox and my hero. He still is. To see him carted off in tears was heartbreaking, genuinely. The anger came with the realisation that he'd been injured on somebody else's time. As I grew older and witnessed the abuse Rangers players would receive when playing for Scotland, I started questioning whether it was worth it.

When we won, it was a fantastic feeling; yet I couldn't wait to get out of Parkhead and head back to Ibrox to watch the players celebrate there. It wasn't our home. Parkhead really was a pit back then, and there was the faint but unmistakable whiff of slumming it as we watched our players cavort with the trophy. It had been a remarkable season, and Rangers deserved all the plaudits they garnered that summer. The sense of expectation was enormous; we simply couldn't wait to have another crack at this Champions League thing. After all, it had seemed quite straightforward this year. Not for the last time, it would prove to be a false dawn.

7

Touched by Genius

For every action, there is an equal and opposite reaction. Or, to put it in a more Scottish context, if you get hammered, you'll have a hangover. Season 1993–94 was one almighty hangover for Rangers after what had turned out to be a champagne season previously. It started so well. We drew Bulgarian champions Levski Sofia in the Champions League qualifier, which, I admit, I thought was a formality. I was not alone in this. This was just before the internet meant you knew everything about every team you are due to play around 15 seconds after drawing them. We operated back then on the British system of 'have we heard of them?' This system meant that drawing Valencia would mean that all conversations would centre around how tough this game was going to be, how they were a good side and how we may struggle. If we drew Villarreal, however, then the chat would be how straightforward the tie would be. The basis for these decisions was purely on the club. You may not know the identity of any players who played for either team, but it didn't matter; therefore, the fact that Levski Sofia were not CSKA Sofia augured well for us.

We won the first leg 3–2 without playing that well. The fans – and I was definitely one of them – saw this match as an annoyance, something to be endured before we could get to the proper football. It was a harsh lesson about taking things for granted. The away goals always looked likely to cause us a bit of a headache, and so it proved. In Sofia we were drawing 1–1 in injury-time. Again, it wasn't on the telly, and I remember listening to the game on radio. Radio is just the worst possible way to experience football. Actually, that's not fair; there is something evocative about listening to football on the radio if it isn't your team that is involved in the match. If it is, then it is torture. Every time the opposition get the ball it seems like they are bearing down mob-handed on our goalkeeper with the rest of our team hopelessly caught upfield. Then there is the dilemma about whether to follow the commentator or the crowd. The commentator tries manfully, but he's always about one nano-second behind the crowd noise. In this match I had endured 90 minutes of sheer undiluted knife-edge trauma before Levski won a corner from which Sofia scored to knock us out of Europe. In August. It felt like being invited back for coffee by an attractive lady then refused entry at the door of the flat.

The season, even at that point, just seemed to stretch out interminably ahead of us. It looked drab. Aberdeen were still our main challengers, but only the most deluded Red thought they would actually win the bloody thing. Celtic were just awful. Liam Brady had left, to be replaced by Lou Macari. Macari had spent most of his career in England and still pops up every year in the papers to tell us how Scotland isn't producing decent players any more. He's been giving the same interview since 1985. Lou's commitment to the biggest job he would ever have could be measured by his refusal to move to Scotland. He'd come up for a couple of days each week, take in the game and then head back home. Nice work if you can get it. Alas, Celtic continued to play poorly during his tenure, despite a shock 2–1 win at Ibrox after a characteristic Ally Maxwell gaffe. Our biggest challenge, as it turned out, would come from ourselves. Simply put, if Rangers played well, we won. If we played something approximating well, we won. Sometimes we were out and out rubbish and we still won. Our players sensed this, and instinctively it had an effect on performances.

How could it not? Everyone in Scottish football may have had different hopes about who would win the League, but they shared the same expectation – it would be Rangers. The other teams took great enjoyment from our miserable European failure – as they would several more times in the remainder of the decade – but who could blame them? It was the only bright light on the horizon for most of them.

The season was memorable for a few things, however. First was Ally McCoist's comeback from his broken leg. He was included in the squad for the League Cup Final against Hibs, with Walter admitting he was nowhere near match fit. But his Roy of the Rovers-like ability to find the net in the big matches meant the script was written for him to go out and score the winner. And, of course, when he appeared as a sub with the game tied at 0–0, it seemed almost inevitable that he would score. Typical McCoist, it was a superb overhead kick into the bottom corner that won the match.

There's a joy in having a player who doesn't let you down when it comes to the big matches. Players who can pop up with vital goals at vital times and do it regularly enough that you rely on them breed confidence in the fans. In truth, Ally was never the same player after the injury. He was always good for goals but was plagued by niggling injuries for the rest of his 'Gers career. Seeing him on the park was always settling, though. You just sort of assumed he would grab a goal at one point.

The other incidents of note came at the tail end of the season. The first was Duncan Ferguson's 'headbutt' in April 2004 on Raith Rovers player John McStay, which resulted in a 12-match SFA ban and, eventually, a six-week stay in Barlinnie Prison. It seemed a bit of a 'handbags' incident, and these days you'd be stunned if the police got involved in an incident of this nature happening on a football field. It should be remembered, however, that Ferguson was on probation for a few previous violent incidents at the time. The police could, and did, argue that it was important to deal with Ferguson's on-field antics as it offered more proof that he had anger-management issues (I believe the colloquial term is 'went radge') that he

73

struggled to control. It was a good bit of PR for the cops, to be fair, as here was a simple bit of routine policing that let them show how tough they were on crime. You could argue whether the streets were any safer with the Dundonian pigeon-fancier in jail. Did it warrant a prison sentence? On its own, no. With the other offences considered? It was still a bit harsh. But still, he'd got himself into the situation.

What was disturbing was the SFA's haste to hit him with a ban, thus finding him guilty of the offence during the concurrent police investigation and completely ignoring the laws of sub-judice. How the SFA could argue that their decision to award him a 12-game suspension didn't prejudice the criminal proceedings is a matter for historians schooled in the absurd. It effectively said, 'He did this; the regulators of his own sport said as much.' Many Rangers fans felt this was more evidence of the SFA being out to get us, but I couldn't bring myself to believe that. This, to me, was an example of muddle-headed SFA decision-making at its finest. One needs to remember that those in charge of our game often make decisions according to the following syllogism:

We need to do something.
This is something.
Therefore we must do this.

The merits of the decision to people like this are not as important as the actual taking of the decision in the first place. It's all tied in with being seen to offer effective leadership as opposed to actually offering effective leadership. Once the decision is made, no matter how unfair, wrong or stupid it turns out to be, it must be rigidly adhered to in the face of any and all criticism, argument or logic. Bouncers follow a similar code of practice.

The other major talking point of this season was that David Murray banned Celtic supporters from attending the last Old Firm match of the season at Ibrox in April 1994. This was due to the fact that the away support had broken a number of seats in the previous match at Ibrox that season and their club had refused to pay for the damage. This was probably due to the Hoops being utterly skint more than any great moral reason. Their board were more and more resembling the Keystone Kops in their attempts at running the place. However, Murray had decided that he would play a populist card, and it certainly was popular. It seemed a great idea; no Tims to pollute the fine air of the South Side. In practice though, it wasn't as much fun as it sounded. You need opposition fans to help create an atmosphere. Without another support to play off, Ibrox was strangely flat. When John Collins scored the opener for Celtic, the whole stadium was silent. The adversity seemed to inspire a pretty rotten Celtic team, who held on for a creditable draw. The SFA introduced a rule which outlawed the banning of away fans by any club. It was an experiment, and it stands as a testimony of when Rangers had a motivated chairman. He probably got that one wrong, in retrospect, but it was a brave move.

I should probably mention that Celtic had a new owner by this juncture. The Bank of Scotland informed Celtic that it was calling in the receivers on Thursday 3 March 1994 as a result of exceeding a £5 million overdraft. However, expatriate businessman Fergus McCann wrested control of the club, and ousted the family dynasties that had controlled Celtic since its foundation. According to media reports, McCann took over the club as little as 18 minutes before it was to be declared bankrupt. Oh, how we laughed.

I'll be honest; I didn't really want Celtic to go bust. Who would we have our rivalry against? Aberdeen? No chance. Partick Thistle? Doesn't do it for me. Scottish football is two big clubs and 38 diddy teams. This is perhaps a little simplistic, but I don't expect this book to form the basis of anyone's PhD thesis soon. We need Celtic as Holmes needed his Moriarty and Superman needed his Lex Luthor. Without Celtic there as a representative of everything that is wrong with the world, how can we effectively demonstrate all that is good and true?

We didn't win the treble thanks to a goalkeeping fankle by Ally Maxwell against Dundee United in the Final. In truth, we'd downed tools after the League was won in March and couldn't pick them back up for the Final. It was a disappointing end to what had been a weird wee season. We had clinched six-in-a-row, however, and talk was really turning to getting nine. Or even 10. Celtic had won nine titles in a row under Jock Stein from 1965–74, and we'd never been allowed to forget it. Now was our chance. Anything they could do, we could do better. Apart from the European Cup, obviously, but as previously discussed that was a fluke we don't recognise round our way.

Summer 1994 was very interesting. We made two major signings – European Cup-winner and Van Basten-nobbler Basile Boli and Danish winger Brian Laudrup. Strange to report now, but we were probably more taken with Basile at the time. Laudrup was a winger who had impressed when playing for Denmark and had a great track record, but he was primarily known as Michael's younger brother. Andy Goram was also placed on the transfer list. Smith had felt he hadn't worked hard enough to get fit at the end of last season and had left us with the unreliable Maxwell. Goram knuckled down and was allowed to stay, but no one really believed Smith would have sold the goalie.

As for the Prince of Denmark, he is simply the finest player I have ever witnessed in a Rangers jersey. A signed picture of him hangs in my house. The guy was a genius with a football, he could speak five languages and he looked cool. A smitten Jim White once asked him 'Brian, why are you so good?' I can understand where Jim was coming from. Laudrup could make the ball sing. He glided effortlessly all over Scottish football for three glorious years and he made you excited when you got up in the morning, never mind when he got the ball. He was just a sublime footballer. Debate rages over who is the greatest foreign player to grace Scottish football. It's fairly simple; Rangers fans will say Laudrup and Celtic fans will say Larsson. It's a bit pointless running through the arguments because it's a subjective debate and no one's opinion will ever change on it. However, it was Laudrup. End of. No argument, it was.

Boli was just brilliant. Not at football, sadly, but as a character. He was huge, like a black Ram-Man from *He-man and the Masters of the Universe*. He kicked a lot of people and was, bizarrely, shunted out to right-back on occasion, despite being slightly less mobile than a mobile disco. He swanned around Glasgow having his picture taken and accepting drinks from strangers. He was cool but, bloody hell, him and Gough at centre-back was a pairing straight from the seventh level of hell.

It cost us immediately. We lost 2–0 to AEK Athens in Greece to give ourselves a mountain to climb to reach the Champions League. It was getting beyond a joke. The Rangers hype machine went into overdrive for the second leg. Gerry McNee tipped us to win 5–0, for God's sake. We narrowly failed to achieve that scoreline, losing 1–0. Beware of Greeks bearing tactical awareness. We were a bloody shambles that night. Smith had picked Ferguson and Hateley up front, a combination that never worked as we tended to simply lump the ball up to the pair of them.

As awful starts go, we decided to go for it. Celtic beat us 2–0 at Ibrox. We then went out of the League Cup, at home to Falkirk. This period was forever known as Rangers' Bad Week. We just looked hopeless. Whether through sheer bloody-mindedness or not, we stepped up a level in the next few weeks. It wasn't pretty, but the results started to flow, although watching the Champions League grow from strength to strength without us was really starting to hurt. There is nothing worse than hearing *Zadok the Priest* and knowing you won't be listening to it at your home stadium. Celtic, thankfully, ran to our early-season rescue. When it seemed that they couldn't fail to finally win a trophy by defeating tiny Raith Rovers at Ibrox in the League Cup Final, they made a howling arse of the match and ended up drawing with the Kirkcaldy team. It went to penalties, with Paul McStay missing what would have been the match-winning kick. The Rangers support collectively wet themselves laughing. At the time I joked that it was almost as good as Rangers winning it. A decade later, when trophies were scarcer than quality programming on STV, I began to realise how much I'd taken the good times for granted.

That season was all about one man, a handsome Dane called Laudrup. The guy was dynamite. Having watched Cooper and Walters, I appreciated good wing play. Those who'd witnessed McLean, Henderson and Johnston did too. But Laudrup, even against those names, was something very special. Unlike most wingers, he didn't flit in and out of play. He was constantly involved and as integral to the team as any midfield player. He immediately began to supply Hateley with the type of crosses that were meat and drink to the big man, who also had an excellent season. But it was the elegance, the sheer beauty he created when he got the ball. He twisted and turned defenders until they were dizzy, he strode past people at pace with the ball mesmerically stuck to his boot. He was lithe, graceful and magnificent. We played Celtic at Hampden early in the season – Parkhead was being redeveloped from the outdated hellhole it was then to the modern hellhole it is now – and he ripped both the heart from and the piss out of them. They just couldn't cope, especially as we also had a centre-half pairing of Boli and Fraser Wishart that day, and the fans had a new hero to laud. We won 3–1, going on six or seven, and it was nice to put them back in their place after our awful performance in the 2–0 defeat in August, when Celtic were miles better than us. Hateley ragdolled their defenders, and I remember the away end just oozing superiority. We were so much better than them, it was untrue. Celtic by now had Tommy Burns in charge after he'd done well as manager of Kilmarnock. We were still four-square behind the man in the cardie, Walter Smith. Walter's sleeveless cardigan was Scottish football's most talked about knitwear for several seasons. He could carry it off; I'm not sure many others could.

It would be remiss not to mention one of the most celebrated incidents of Scottish football folklore that took place this season. Chic Young had been sent to interview Walter about Rangers' exit from Europe. He proceeded to misread a clearly stewing Walter and was met with a volley of abuse from the mild-mannered 'Gers boss, which also included the assistant manager, Archie Knox, suggesting he was a particularly unpleasant, if functional, body part. Walter indignantly asked Young if he knew anything about football, which seemed a rhetorical question. It's on YouTube, have a look. Chic is a good example of a particularly BBC creation, the exalted status of the people they employ who have been around for so long that the Beeb assume they must be considered 'national treasures'. In some cases – Bruce Forsyth, say – it's true. In other cases, like Chic Young, it really isn't. I have never met a football fan, of any persuasion, who didn't think Chic Young was a runt. At least, that's what the word they used sounded like. He appears to have an inordinately high opinion of his status in the game when all he's done for three decades is stand at the side of the park asking stupid questions and giving the teams. But fair play to him, he's made a little talent go a long way. Actually, I'm not sure what that talent is, so his longevity is even more impressive.

We strolled the League again, our seventh League title in a row, and by now the focus was on winning nine. Celtic had improved throughout the course of the season under Burns and would eventually win the Scottish Cup that season. The talk from Parkhead started to emanate about how nine would be a pipedream. There was always a hint of desperation to the bravado, though. The juggernaut seemed to be moving along towards the eventuality, and nobody had been able to leave a glove on us. Motherwell were our nearest challengers, for goodness sake. But having gone from a treble, to a double, to one trophy in three seasons, there was an unease among the support. We'd had no Champions League football for two seasons and, Laudrup aside, there was a shortage of creative quality players at the club.

For me personally it was stage two as a Rangers fan. I was going to university, was no longer a kid and had started to read one of the fanzines sold outside the ground, a wee publication called *Follow Follow*. It was an eye-opener for me. The feelings of disquiet I had were routinely shushed in the official publications. The *Rangers News* exists as a sort of benign *Pravda* for the club. Nothing is ever bad in the land of the official club publication. The matchday programme is a great example. If you were to read a programme from 1985, 1995 and 2005 you'd be most struck by **79** how similar they are – it's really only the names of the players that change. The club magazine is exactly the same. 'I'm coming back to fitness,' says Player X. 'We were disappointed by the performance but we all need to get up for this week's game,' says Player Y. These are two staples of the *News*. Same old, week in, week out, a column by Derek Johnstone that says nothing and there's your two quid.

That said, I don't actually have a problem with it. The official club publication is not going to differ much in opinion from those at the top of the tree. Rangers' mission statement for the last decade seems to have been 'keep calm and carry on,' as every slight, issue or uncomfortable problem is routinely ignored in the heartfelt (if usually unrewarded) hope that it will go away. In those circumstances your job is to batter out a magazine that doesn't bother anybody and doesn't cause any hassle. What I admire is the way Celtic operates theirs. Yes, I said it. Celtic use their club magazine to talk to their fans. I'm not naïve – the fans are being given the message that their board want them to get. But witness season 2009–10, when Celtic tried to push the idea that it was down to the bastard refs that they were losing the title rather than a poor side led by a dire manager. The *Celtic View* was full of it. Editorials ran on how unfair it all was. The message was rubbish, but their fans lapped it up. It bought Mowbray another three months and bought Peter Lawell enough space to play what should have been his trump card in Robbie Keane. The fans were also getting something they couldn't find elsewhere, as even the papers in Scotland couldn't really go along with the whole 'it's a conspiracy' thing, much as some of them wanted to. That's what a club magazine is for – not for an article with Davie Weir where he talks about 'guiding the young lads' three times a season.

Follow Follow was funny, direct and it took the piss. Scottish football is humourless; Scottish football fans are not. The media do enjoy a pious wringing of the hands now and again. The seriousness with which the game is taken up here is simply preposterous. I've been hung up many times for taking the mickey out of people on the radio. It's just not the done thing. Humour is feared, and I'm not sure who made that decision. As I read the articles bemoaning things like our scattergun transfer policy, European failure and lack of youngsters breaking through into the first team, I began to feel a kindred spirit out there. Of course, I didn't know just how big an impact that wee magazine would have on my life.

8

It'll Never be Nine in a Row

1995 was the summer of Britpop and Gazza. Blur, Oasis and a hundred indie chancers with 60s songbooks took over the charts, while Rangers went rock'n'roll in their own way by signing the most famous British player they could. Paul Gascoigne was coming back to Britain with a lot to prove. Italia '90 was a fading memory and the guy's career was stalled in Italy. He announced he would be returning home, but I never gave it a moment's thought. He was an English creation, and they were fascinated by him. There seemed no way he'd end up plying his trade in Scotland. Of course, that didn't stop the papers linking us with him, but as previously noted that didn't really mean much. They linked us with everybody, even if it was just 'an interest'. This is a bored football journalist's get-out-of-jail-free card when they have nothing to write. Call up a manager and say 'would you be interested in Lionel Messi?' 'Of course,' says the manager, 'but there are a hundred factors to consider that would make the move impossible.' The journalist politely notes his comments then ignores them, while splashing a story of no substance under a massive banner header saying 'Club Interested in Messi'. It's a wee bit true but is actually mainly bollocks. It sells papers.

These stories started getting stronger until it was clear we were in the running for him and then, eventually, it was announced. We'd signed Gazza. The gestation period of the deal had built the excitement levels up and it burst out in a wave of peroxide. Gazza, you see, was bleached blond at the time, and soon so was half of Glasgow. Of course, he was hot off the plane from four years in Rome and had a tan; the Glasgow blondes were hot off a sunbed and looked mahogany. Never mind sectarianism, the over-tanning of this nation is Scotland's real secret shame.

We'd signed a few other players, including Oleg Salenko, a barrel-chested Russian who was a good finisher but ran like he needed a hip replacement. Even so, we looked ready to do something at long last in Europe and actually qualified for the tournament after eliminating the mighty Anorthosis Famagusta of Cyprus in the qualifier. It was not easy, though. We won 1–0 over two of the tensest, dreariest games you can imagine. Dull didn't cover it, but it didn't matter. We were on our way.

We started slowly, while Celtic, somewhat shockingly given the previous decade, weren't rubbish. It took a readjustment of one's attitude to get used to that. Burns had signed some really decent players, including Andy Thom, one of the few Celtic players I sneakingly had a regard for. He was a great player.

Gazza mania was running wild in Scotland, and the papers couldn't believe their good luck. The guy was manna from heaven for slow news days. There was a thrilling article about him buying a fish supper and equally exciting one about him ordering expensive wine with his dinner at the hotel he was staying at. These stories both made the front page. I am not joking. Basically, if the guy passed wind, the Scottish press sent a team out to cover it. The justification was that the fans wanted to know this stuff. It's a false premise. No one ever asks fans if they are interested in fluff like this because they know the answer would be a resounding 'No'.

I felt sorry for Gazza. He was thrust into a media glare from an early age and then poked and prodded to try to get a reaction. When a reaction was forthcoming, the press oohed and ahhed and pretended that it was some major event. The poor man never got any peace. Our old friend Gerry McNee got on his case right from the start, refusing to call him by his name and instead calling him 'Number 8' after his shirt number. It was a snivelling, cowardly attempt to dehumanise him. When you won't even give someone the basic courtesy of calling them by their name, it reveals a deep personal issue. Nobody quite knows why McNee was so dismissive of Gascoigne. His off-field behaviour? As time has shown, Gascoigne has a lot of mental health and substance issues. He seems someone deserving of sympathy, but he was a Rangers player, so that was out the window. Instead he was pilloried pretty much from the start because he was a young, working-class guy with very little education who occasionally acted in the way that thousands of people act. The stench of bitterness, jealousy and hypocrisy from McNee's weekly rants about him was overpowering and sad.

He got into trouble after his debut in a friendly at Ibrox when he mimed playing a flute after scoring a goal. This was a celebration that had been mischievously recommended to him by other players and Gazza, always desperate to fit in and to be liked, performed it. The papers reacted like he'd taken a dump in the grotto at Lourdes and scribbled 'UDA' in it. He was guilty of bigotry, you see. He could have started a riot. Except, of course, he couldn't. He did it in a friendly at Ibrox where the crowd was almost exclusively Rangers' fans. And, apart from that, so what? He mimicked an Orange Order flautist. As far as I know, the Orange Order is not an illegal organisation. You may not agree with what they do or why they exist — I'm not a member and have no interest in it — but it is a legitimate organisation and I can't recall it being involved in any terrorist atrocities. So what's the problem?

We beat Celtic 2–0 at Parkhead early that season, with Gascoigne scoring the second. The cameras caught a charge of Celtic fans running down the stairs at Parkhead to the front of the stands to wave their scarves at him as he celebrated. This was standard operating procedure for Celtic fans for a while. In times of trouble, they would wave their scarves at opposition players. The reasons behind this were never made clear. I'm not sure if they thought that this gesture would make the player realise the futility of scoring against Celtic, perhaps plant a seed of doubt in his mind the next time he ran through on goal – 'I'd better not score this, they might wave their scarves at me again.' What was frightening with Gascoigne, however, was the sheer, unbridled hatred on their faces. They despised Gascoigne. This, of course, just made us love him more.

Gascoigne was different to Laudrup. Laudrup exuded European cool; Gazza certainly did not. He was a bit tubby and a bit wild, but the things the guy could do with a ball at his feet were incredible. Watching him in full flight and in top form was a privilege. He could beat a man with ease, his passing was superb and he scored some outrageous goals. He was the epitome of the phrase 'wearing his heart on his sleeve'. The support could identify with the man because he played football the way we did when we were kids; 100 miles an hour, always wanting the ball, trying to do things no one else on the park would dream of. His emotion was never far from the surface, and we adopted him as our family maverick.

He started slowly, perhaps understandably because of his injury history and the weight of expectation around him. The Champions League that year became, very quickly, a very painful reality check. We lost our opening game against Steaua Bucharest after trying to defend for 90 minutes and being undone by a wonder goal in the last minute. We drew 2–2 with Borussia Dortmund in a great match at Ibrox, played in a surreal atmosphere. Rangers had decided to charge the ludicrous price of £100 for tickets to the three home matches. The fans voted with their feet. It was too much money to ask people to part with. Rangers had to listen and eventually realised you would be better selling 50,000 tickets at £80 than 30,000 at £100. We then ran into Juventus, beaten finalists the year before, the team who would go on to win it that year and lose in the Final the following year. They were scarily good. Packed with talent including Vialli,

Ravanelli and Del Piero, they didn't have a weakness. Their players were also absolutely massive. Juve were later implicated in a doping scandal, and to be fair, it's not tough to believe that some of the physiques on display were chemically enhanced. When we walked in and watched them warming up, my Dad turned to me and said, 'We could be in trouble here, son.' He wasn't wrong. Due to the three-foreigner rule, we had Gary Bollan playing. Gary could never have been accused of performance-enhancing drug use. They had a team of gazelles who were stronger than horses, and technically they were superb. They murdered us 4–0, and it could have been far more. Charlie Miller did miss a sitter for us at 1–0, but I think that might just have annoyed them. There was a good bit of banter at half-time. Both teams had suffered poor defeats in the recent weeks before the match; we'd been knocked out of the League Cup by Aberdeen and they'd been stuffed 4–0 by Lazio in the live Channel 4 match the Sunday before. Desperate for any bit of comfort, the home support started chanting '4–0 to the Lazio' only to be met with an accented 'Aberdeen, Aberdeen, Aberdeen' (undoubtedly the only time that word will be heard in connection with the Champions League.) The ref mercifully put us out of our misery but then it dawned on us; we'd have to go over there in two weeks. Well, we improved dramatically, and, in one of those fairytale matches, only lost 4–1. To say we were outplayed is like saying John Prescott likes cakes. They were a magnificent team, and our European tactics at the time – basically, give the ball to Paul and Brian and hope they do something – didn't manage to knock them off their path.

A 1–1 draw with Steaua, notable only for a wonderful individual goal from Gazza, finished us off before we managed a creditable 2–2 draw with Dortmund in the magnificent Westfalenstadion. We were out without managing a win in six matches. This, no matter how you try to spin it, was a poor campaign. Luckily, our exit coincided with a great run of form, culminating in a 7–0 win over Hibs, which was one of the best performances from a Rangers team I have witnessed. It was also pleasing to stick seven past Jim Leighton, who made it pretty obvious during his time with Aberdeen that he didn't care for us, and who some Reds ludicrously claimed was better than Andy Goram. This is a bit like me saying I'm a better writer than Norman Mailer. His shell-shocked face when leaving the pitch was a testament to the blitz he'd just endured. This was also the game in which Gazza was booked for jokingly showing the referee the yellow card as he returned it to him after the ref, Dougie Smith, had dropped it. I have no doubts that this would not have happened to any other player. The ref was at Defcon 3 when dealing with Gazza, so he was aware of the possibility for criticism if he failed to deal properly with him. This went back to a draw with Aberdeen in a fiery match at Ibrox that year when Gascoigne, fed up of being fouled constantly, lost his rag and nutted an Aberdeen player in the chest, Zidane style. He should have been sent off but wasn't, and after that his card was marked. Smith was a weaselly-looking wee man. His career effectively ended that day, and so it should have.

I've often wondered about match officials. Not referees, but linesmen. I can see why some people might want to be refs; it's perfect for people who were bullied, or have an officious streak they want to give free reign to. I always thought Gerry McNee would have made a good ref if he wasn't so grotesquely fat. But linesmen…what sort of human being wants to do that? You stand on the wing waving your flag and getting abused by thousands of people. As a fan, an unbeatable joy at the match is noticing the linesman on your side is either bald or fat. This will provide much ammunition over the course of the next 90 minutes. You can, for example, go for the old classic 'How did ye no see that? Hair in yer eyes?' You can also say, 'Try to keep up son – imagine the ball is a sausage roll.' This will cause much mirth and annoy the linesman. Though be careful where and when you do this. My cousin Alex spent a large part of a Kilwinning Rangers match abusing the rotund linesman only for the guy to turn round, throw his flag down and offer him a square go in the car park. Alex, who couldn't fight sleep, politely turned down the generous offer to get his head kicked in. Ayrshire Juniors – it's hard core.

Celtic were actually playing really well, too, but this again highlights the differences in perception between the two clubs. Despite having players like Laudrup and Gascoigne and scoring shedloads of goals, we were often labelled defensive. Similarly, Celtic played good, attractive football under Tommy Burns for two of his three years in charge, which was the only time in two decades they have managed to do so, yet they are constantly given the mantle as the true heirs to Real Madrid 1960. But they kept coming at us, and it seemed a given that we would end up going right to the end of the season. This was a special time for British football; Euro '96 was being held in England and Scotland had joined them in qualifying. Indeed, Scotland and England had been drawn together. In England, Kevin Keegan's Newcastle team were on the verge of blowing it against Manchester United in the wake of his 'love it, love it' rant. There were talking points all over the shop.

I had left school and gone to university, and here I began to notice different attitudes among football fans in higher education. There were loads of hooped tops at lectures. It would never have occurred to me to wear a Rangers top to one. I think the desire to let someone know exactly what you are within a nanosecond of meeting them stems from insecurity, and while it's not exactly exclusive to Celtic fans, it's certainly more prevalent. I noticed among my fellow Bears a tendency at uni to apologise for what they were. A sort of 'let's all be friends attitude' fostered by the received wisdom where we were the big bad wolves and these poor wee Celtic fans had spent years under the yoke of our oppression. I thought it was bollocks then and I think its bollocks now. I was a Rangers fan and I didn't think any less of you for not being one, though if you were calling me a bigot and assigning me a nice wee pigeon-hole a few minutes after meeting me, simply because I was a Rangers fan, you clearly thought less of me. Sometimes those who see bigotry everywhere they turn might find it's because they carry it around with them.

This was the season that Rangers developed a signature style against Celtic: the opposition would have the lion's share of possession, we would defend heroically and our goalkeeper would be inspired. Then we would score on the break and hold out resolutely for the win. It was a tactical masterclass from Walter and it worked so often that it prompted Tommy Burns to say his gravestone would have the words 'Andy Goram broke my heart' inscribed upon it. We really did have their measure, and it proved crucial as both teams achieved a level of consistency that meant the head-to-heads would prove crucial. We also beat them in the Scottish Cup semi-final 2–1, thanks to goals from McCoist and Laudrup. Add in McCoist's winner in the League Cup at Parkhead, and it meant we had eliminated them from the two Cups. Now all we had to do was win the League.

It came down to a match against Aberdeen at Ibrox in May 1996. A win and we would win the League for the eighth time in a row. Anything else meant it carried on until the last game of the season. Aberdeen were not the red-clad joke they are now. They had some good players and they always gave us a game. Sure enough, they took the lead in front of an expectant, if jumpy, crowd. Step forward Paul Gascoigne. In one of the best individual displays I have ever seen, he took the game by the scruff of the neck. He equalised in the first half with a lovely bit of skill and good finish, but that was just the starter. The main course was his second – receiving the ball in his own half, he ran the length of the park, holding off a posse of Aberdeen defenders before delicately passing the ball into the far corner of the net. It was a sublime goal, an absolute gem. He then finished with the dessert – a penalty for his hat-trick after Gordon Durie had been fouled. We were the champions again.

I can't let the season end without mentioning the Laudrup Cup Final of May 1996. We beat Hearts 5–1, and despite Gordon Durie scoring a hat-trick everyone remembers Lauder's sensational display that day. He tore them to shreds. The really pleasing thing was that Hearts had humped us twice in the League that season and were unbelievably cocky going into the match. It was nice to put them so firmly in their place.

Euro '96 was fun. It was the first time I had been of legal age to take advantage of the various beer deals that seem to pop up during major competitions. And Scotland were good! We kicked off with a creditable goalless draw against a Dutch side that had some superb players, though were later revealed to be riven with internal strife. Still, any point against the Dutch is always a good result. Next up, England. Craig Brown didn't start with Ally McCoist, which was a blunder. With the score at 1–0 to England, Scotland won a penalty, which Gary McAllister missed. Ally would have scored. This is a fact. England then went up the park and Gazza scored that wonder goal where he flipped the ball over Colin Hendry before volleying it past Andy Goram. The pub in Kilwinning experienced a bittersweet sensation. Obviously gutted, but still, he was our English bastard. You could spot the Bears by their reaction. After the exclaimed 'Oh, f**k!' came a more reflective 'Some goal, right enough'. McCoist scored a wonderful winner against Switzerland in the next game, but it wasn't enough to prevent our eventual elimination. England looked like they might actually win the bloody thing, but the inevitable Germany plus penalties equals heartbreak equation did for them.

One of the more recent myths of Scottish football is that Rangers fans all support England. This is an assumption based upon the fact that Rangers fans wave British flags – you know, the country we live in – and some wear England tops. First things first – Rangers are a British club and proud of it. Secondly, the Union Flag also matches our club colours. You don't need to be Gok Wan to see how these two facts complement each other. Thirdly, the tops thing. A minute percentage of Rangers fans have done this. Some do it because they are English, some in tribute to our English players, and still do it more to wind up the Hamishes in the Scotland support who don't like us. Celtic fans wear Ireland tops in far more numbers than Rangers fans wear England tops. The vast majority of Rangers fans either support Scotland or don't give a Donald Duck about international football.

My support for Scotland waned simply when I realised it wasn't absolute any more. I don't know how this happened, but I remember watching a game in 1999 against Belgium with my friends Chris

(Kilmarnock fan) and Neal (Aberdeen fan – honestly). When we scored they were elated. I was happy but not ecstatic. Similarly, when Belgium scored a last-minute equaliser I didn't feel the pain quite as acutely as they did. This wasn't a conscious choice. It was just the way I felt. Since then I have attended several Scotland games, and I always hope they win. But I wouldn't consider myself a die-hard. The Tartan Army seem a nice enough bunch, but I'm not one for kilt-wearing unless it's at a wedding. Similarly, the results don't feel like a shot of adrenaline or a boot in the balls to me the way a Rangers result can. There is an old joke about the fan who supports two teams only: Rangers and Rangers reserves. I don't even care how the reserves do. It's similar when people discuss their English team. I quite like Everton, but how they do doesn't keep me up at night. I am a monogamous football fan. And there is no chance of a divorce in this marriage, no matter how badly the other half treats me.

So onwards into 1996–97. A momentous year lay ahead as we chased the holy grail of nine in a row. It started badly, as it usually did, when we were shite in the Champions League. At times it seemed like our players failed to learn anything from their previous experiences. It began badly with a 3–0 defeat to Grasshoppers of Zurich. Gazza kicked a ball at Gerry McNee up in the stand and apparently hit him. McNee claimed Richard Gough, the skipper, apologised to him. I hope this was just a hallucination Gerry suffered due to the trauma of a skelped napper. Apologise? We should have charged him the price of a new football for damaging the old one. The low point came with a 4–0 defeat in Amsterdam to Ajax, which was notable for Gascoigne's red card. Gazza had been all over the papers for beating his wife Sheryl and took it on to the park with him, as they say. We were just as shambolic in the other matches, and ended with one win and five defeats. God bless getting back to the domestic game.

The number nine was everywhere. John Lennon's estate must have made a fortune from the royalties as *#9 Dream* was played every time a Rangers player appeared on camera. Desperation to stop us was nearly visible from Parkhead. It was a season where every match had huge importance. The teams still mostly played at the same time, which meant that, as a fan, you spent the game with a radio pressed up your ear to find out how their game was going. These days it's rare for the Old Firm to play on the same day, never mind the same time. It really added a frisson to the match when you were waiting for some spontaneous outburst from other fans as an indicator that Celtic had conceded.

I knew we were going to win it. This was due to the power of the lucky coat, a Rangers bench jacket manufactured by Adidas, which I had taken to wearing to matches. When I didn't wear it, we drew or lost. My Dad made me wear it for a few seasons no matter what the weather. A hangover is not pleasant in 70-degree heat while swaddled in an anorak, by the way. To this day my old man puts the loss of 10 in a row down to me giving the coat away that pre-season. Never mind that it was falling apart, he's convinced we would have won the Champions League by now if I'd held on to it. We were once listening to an away match against Aberdeen when, from 2–0 up, we were pegged back to 2–2 and reduced to 10 men. He suggested I put the coat on – in the house – for the last 10 minutes. We went on to win 4–2. That is one powerful coat.

Fans are mental that way. Lucky coats, lucky scarves, lucky pubs – we've tried them all. I have friends I won't offer spare tickets to because I am convinced that they are jinxes. This is not sensible behaviour. Football makes us all spiritual, praying to any number of gods for the tiny stroke of fortune that will give us an advantage. It really shouldn't make a difference to the result if I am wearing a particular aftershave, yet I am convinced it does. It really shouldn't matter what I've had for breakfast, but I will not eat Shredded Wheat on a match day, regardless. This game drives you mad, but I'm pretty sure a lot of us are halfway down that road already when we sign up.

Celtic had signed Paolo di Canio in the close season as their answer to Laudrup. Burns had said he was 'born to play for Celtic'. I actually quite liked Paolo. He acted like a colossal bellend, but he could play. And he was always good for a laugh. During an Old Firm game Andy Goram twice booted the ball at him during a break in play behind the ref's back, and he went apeshit. He threatened to break Ian Ferguson's legs, all stereotypical Italian vim and vinegar. He was a bit of a figure of fun, but he did give them something.

The Old Firm games that year decided the League. They were all astonishing. In the opener at Ibrox, Celtic were down to 10 men and a goal down in the last minute when they hit the bar. From the rebound, Gazza hared down the park, played a one-two with Jorg Albertz and bulleted a header home to seal it. He was blonde again, the club having ordered him to get his hair dyed back because they had thousands of unsold t-shirts with his blonde bonce on them, and they wanted help to shift them. The next match at Parkhead had the lot. Brian O'Neill stood on the ball early, which allowed Laudrup to nip through and smash one home for us. After that, it was the usual Goram magnificence before we were awarded a penalty, which Gazza missed. Still we had time for Peter van Vossen, our Dutch striker, to blast the ball over an open goal from 12 yards. It looked like we didn't want to clinch it. This was further reinforced when Celtic were awarded a late penalty. Pierre van Hooijdonk stood up to hit it, only to see Goram — who never saved penalties — save it. My heart had gone about five times in this match alone. Then it was on to the New Year game.

That game came at a bad time for us. We had no Gough or Laudrup due to 'flu, then Gazza succumbed to it during the match. We had taken the lead due to an absolute howitzer of a free-kick from Jorg Albertz – der Hammer – which nearly took the net off the rigging. After that, Celtic battered us. And I mean battered. It looked as though we might pull our party trick of nicking the win, but then di Canio scored. The away end went ballistic, and a lot of them ran on the park, as they always seem to do at Ibrox. I'd hire a sniper and warn them before hand what would happen if any of them made their way on to the field. This may seem harsh, but it would soon put a stop to it. Anyway, we looked buggered. There were 20 minutes to go and us without our key players against a resurgent gang of evildoers with their tails up.

Walter, clearly desperate, sent on van Vossen and Erik Bo Andersen. Erik Bo was a gangly Danish striker who had appeared to be pish. Legend has it he embraced a somewhat alternative lifestyle off the pitch and that his less enlightened teammates had taken exception to it, leaving him allegedly drenched in someone's body fluids after training, and not the one you would expect. Bo came on, but I wasn't overly hopeful.

God was smiling down us that night. Brian O'Neill – him again – got in a fankle on the edge of his box, and Andersen took advantage for 2–1. I remember being swept up into the crowd when it went in and not caring where I landed. Then came a moment Celtic fans still cling to in their belief the world is against them. Jorge Cadete had a goal incorrectly ruled out for offside. Thing was, the linesman was right in front of me, and had his flag up before Cadete knocked it in, so it was never a goal as far as I was concerned. Erik Bo knocked another one in, just to make it funnier. Good times.

The League Cup had been secured in one of the great Finals of our time, a 4–3 win over Hearts at Parkhead. Rangers had been 2–0 up and were cruising before Hearts, inspired by Neil McCann, drew level. McCoist and Gascoigne had a famous set-to leaving the pitch, which led to the cheeky chappy of Scottish football belting the errant Geordie genius on the back of the napper. Whatever he did, it seemed to work, as Gascoigne scored two magnificent solo efforts to secure the Cup. This Final I missed, the first in years and, thankfully, the last for years. Why? I had met a girl, a Celtic fan, and was being introduced her parents. When we got married years later, I reflected that it had been worth it. When we got divorced a few years after that, I wished I'd gone to the game! That's not true. If you are going to miss a Cup Final, then it has to be worth it and I still think this was.

Celtic knocked us out of the Scottish Cup that year. Walter put out what can only be described as a strange team selection, including young defender Craig Moore in midfield, for some reason, and Celtic were two up by half-time and really enjoying it. They had taken to gathering together in a huddle before the match, a tradition that exists to this day. It is, apparently, the most special thing anyone has ever done, ever, and is the envy of all other football fans the world over. Anyway, after cuffing us in the Cup – and they had cuffed us – they performed this huddle after the match in front of the delirious hooped hordes. This was a none-too-subtle 'get it up ye' to us. Fair enough, but every dog has its day and payback is a bitch. I got astonishingly drunk after the match, and ruminated on my Dad's assertion that it wasn't worth getting upset about as empires had formed and buildings had been built and fallen since the last time they beat us. All I knew was that the next day, as I nursed a stinking hangover on the way to uni, I couldn't help but notice how many *Big Issue* sellers were wearing Celtic tops.

This is the first season I can remember Celtic fans performing *You'll Never Walk Alone* with any gusto. Now, according to some of the more deluded and mental Celtic supporters I've shared oxygen with, they had sung this song forever, before Liverpool, before Gerry and the Pacemakers and probably before it featured in *Carousel*. This inability of mine – and everybody else – to recall them using it first can only be down to one of two things. One, a collective failure of memory from everyone who doesn't support Celtic; or two, they are talking out of their arses.

After three League wins against our only serious title challengers, you'd think that the title would have been in the bag, but it wasn't. Celtic were much more consistent against the diddy teams; therefore, it came down to the last Old Firm League match of the season at Parkhead. We were beset by an injury crisis. We always seemed beset by an injury crisis. *Follow Follow* asked what we did in training and suggested that we simply ignored the ball and instead indulged in full-contact games of British Bulldog. There seemed no other explanation. Walter sprung a surprise by re-signing Mark Hateley for the match from QPR. He arrived back saying he felt like he was coming home. We were also without the goalie, and our reserve 'keeper, a Dutchman called Theo Snelders, was flakier than a consignment of flakes destined for Amy Winehouse. Walter brought in veteran goalkeeper Andy Dibble on loan. Things did not look good.

Parkhead that day was feverish. There is no other word for it. We scored the opener from the head of none other than Sir Brian. Then Hateley got sent off after a tussle with Celtic goalkeeper Stewart Kerr. The game seemed to last for about seven hours, but eventually it ended and we had won. The ninth title was ours to lose. We celebrated like mad and our players, remembering the Cup match, performed a mock huddle in front of the away end. This was seized upon by the Celtic management as a wind-up. Well, it was, same as theirs had been a few weeks earlier. If you are going to give it out, you have to take it.

After this match, it was all set for us to win the title at home against Motherwell and, in the true Rangers way, we buggered it up, losing 2–0. This meant we had a tricky away match against Dundee United followed by an even trickier game away to Hearts to get the three points we needed.

The Dundee United game was impossible to get tickets for and, again, wasn't on the telly. I sat in my bedroom with a huge carry-out and died a thousand deaths as I listened to the match. Laudrup, fittingly, got the goal that would bring us the record-equalling ninth title. We had done it. Nine in a row.

Some fans debate about whose nine was better. If you want to break it down into purely factual terms – and I'm sure my answer will surprise you – it was ours. The reason is simply that Rangers had completed theirs in the era of the Premier League. This meant you played the best teams four times a season, rather than twice. Celtic had only had to play everybody twice. However, in the final analysis, it means nothing. Nine is nine and, whenever you managed the feat, it was impressive. You can only beat what is in front of you. What I will say though is that nine was mine. If you are a Celtic fan my age, nine-in-a-row to you is just something from the history books. I lived through our nine, I was there to see every trophy, I sweated and worried and earned the joy of it at the end. That'll do for me.

I worried about 10. The focus to get nine had been so big, there was an underlying sense that we had achieved what we had set out to do. This

Myself and my sister Ann with a Mafioso-style Uncle Tam.

With the family, my mum looking thoughtful.

Ann and I watching the Marseilles game, 1993.

Celebrating my birthday with cousins Steven and Bryan.

Tenth birthday, wearing the only gifts I wanted.

Christmas Day 1992 – Rangers bathrobe, oh yes!.

The Nike family day at Ibrox. We beat ourselves 6–1.

Me, Ann and Dad.

Me in Nashville.

Me at work, reviewing a gig.

The bust of Bill Struth on the Marble Staircase.

ERECTED BY
WILLIAM STRUTH
IN LOVING MEMORY OF
HIS DEAR WIFE
CATHERINE FORBES
WHO DIED 22ᴺᴰ DECEMBER 1941
ALSO THE ABOVE
WILLIAM STRUTH
MANAGER OF
RANGERS FOOTBALL CLUB
1920 - 54
WHO DIED 21ˢᵀ SEPTEMBER 1956

The grave of a great man.

Ibrox Stadium. Home.

The trophy cabinet at Ibrox.

Some of the hundreds of pennants which adorn the trophy room walls.

In the home dressing room. Davie Weir is older than me. There's still hope.

Ibrox from the tunnel.

Ibrox from the pitch.

Barry Ferguson collects the 2008 League Cup (picture by Alan Jones).

Kris Boyd scores the winning penalty in the 2008 League Cup Final (picture by Alan Jones).

Brothers in Arms. Ian, Scot, me and Dad in the Ritz, Manchester.

Scot and I fly the flag in Manchester.

Me, Stuart and Iain in Picadilly Square. Note me drinking Iain's lager. Classy chick.

Nothing's gonna stop us now…except Zenit.

The teams emerge, UEFA Cup Final 2008. I'm crying as I took this, by the way.

The fans, UEFA Cup Final 2008.

Our view at the UEFA Cup Final 2008.

Davie Weir leads the players off the field after the 2008 UEFA Cup Final (picture by Colin Robertson).

Ally salutes the fans after the 2008 UEFA Cup Final (picture by Colin Robertson).

worried me, but I shoved it to the back of my mind. Richard Gough announced he was going to play in America and Brian Laudrup was announced as our new captain. We bought a lot of players for big money, including the Italian contingent of Lorenzo Amoruso, Sergio Porrini and Marco Negri. We'd also signed an unknown youngster called Rino Gattuso. Whatever happened to him? We were, however, overcome by hubris. We had a 'family day' before the season started where we showed off our massive squad by having the 'blues' play the 'whites'. Worryingly, the blues won 6–1.

That season was awful. We just fell apart. The squad was old and tired. We didn't even make the Champions League for our ritual humiliation, being humped by Gothenburg in the qualifier. This meant we went into the UEFA Cup. We buggered that up too, losing 4–2 on aggregate to a deeply average Strasbourg team. In European terms, we were rotten. And, for once, the League didn't offer any solace. Brian Laudrup, the best player I have ever seen, had a dire season. He was out of contract at the end of the year and already looking at his next move, if his performances were anything to go by. Gazza was, we would later find out, having serious alcohol issues. He was sold to Middlesbrough in March. Negri started like a train, scoring 30-odd goals by Christmas. He hit all five in a 5–1 win over Dundee United early in the season. However, he was involved in a mysterious incident while playing squash with Sergio Porrini and suffered an eye injury that seemed to rule him out of playing for us permanently. Wee Rino became a cult hero for his no-nonsense tackling, including an assault on Tom Boyd in an Old Firm match. But we were poor. Injuries ripped us apart and our so-called 'super squad' proved to be much more about quantity than quality. Celtic had appointed a tightly-permed Dutchman called Wim Jansen as a replacement for the talented but flawed management of Burns, to howls of laughter from us. But Jansen was pragmatic. The team he built wasn't a patch on Burns', but they didn't bugger up the games against the smaller sides. Although we kept beating them that season – including two wins in a week, late in the season, one to knock them out of the Cup – we just weren't able to sustain it. They won the League on the last day to foil 10. They probably deserved it.

Walter had announced in December that this was to be his last campaign and he was leaving at the end of the season. It seemed to symbolise the ennui that gripped the place. The old guard, the players who had been there for the long-haul, knew that they would be leaving too. It was a strange atmosphere to be working towards such a milestone. That it didn't happen was a source of huge frustration. I think this was one of the first times that a schism appeared between Murray and the fans, small though it was. He expected to be remembered as the guy who had brought us nine; many fans felt he'd failed to deliver 10. Hyper-critical? Probably. I admit during the 1990s I felt that we won the League by rote and that anything less was rank failure. After a few lean seasons I began to realise that this had been a golden era for us Bears.

We'd run the white flag up when we'd sold Gazza. His alcohol intake was massive, he wasn't training properly and there had been an incident during his warm up as sub in the 2–0 defeat at Parkhead when he had played the invisible flute again. The first time was excusable, the second time was not. The media gleefully took him to task for this. Davie Provan suggested that Gazza's actions could damage the Northern Irish peace process. While we can safely write off the opinion of the Sky Henry Kissinger, it was a daft gesture when he knew what the probable outcome was. Rangers sold him in March. A visibly distraught Gazza was paraded at Middlesbrough. Even out of form and unfit, he should have been kept. Losing him was a hammer blow to the fans' morale.

There was the small matter of the Scottish Cup Final to come. Our season had really hit it's nadir in the third round against Dundee, when the First Division side had held us to a 0–0 draw. For the replay we had half a team missing, but a double from the old warhorse McCoist took us through. Ally was superb during that second half of the season. He just refused to see us lose and through sheer force of will almost propelled us to the double. It was a hell of an effort from a 36-year-old, and it summed the guy up. He's a legend, pure and simple.

Hearts awaited us, and this time we fell short. We lost 2–1 in a game chiefly remembered for two penalty decisions, one for us, one against. Stevie Fulton was fouled on the halfway line by Ian Ferguson, and ref Willie Young gave a penalty. In the second half, substitute McCoist – shamefully left out of the starting XI – had got us back in it with a typical Coisty goal. We were chasing an equaliser when Ally was upended in the box. Young waved away the claims and Hearts had won a trophy for the first time since Christopher Columbus was cutting about the high seas. I'm not one for thinking referees are bent. In Scotland, I just think they are bad. But Willie Young was an arsehole. He revelled in giving controversial decisions against us. Earlier that season he had sent Amoruso off at Pittodrie for shoving Eoin Jess in the chest. The following season, he gave a penalty against Andrei Kanchelskis for standing there while Andy Smith jumped, then bolted over to our dug-out to send Dick Advocaat to the stand. It was probably the fastest time the pie-lover ran in his whole life. He was a joke, and his decisions were so awful and so often that it was hard to put it down to just sheer incompetence. While I've disliked many refs, he's the only one I ever felt we were playing 12 men with.

So, a valedictory wave to the support and that was that. We had a new manager, the aforementioned Advocaat. We had a clean slate and a new start. Little did I know that the next three years would be the start of the journey that would coincide with the chairman calling me a nonentity on the telly.

9

The Oranje Order

Dick Advocaat arrived with an amusing name and a sterling reputation. He'd been announced as the new manager in January and since then his every move had been analysed by the press. He was painted as a tough disciplinarian with an eye for detail and a passion for passing football. He announced that he'd be bringing his captain at PSV with him, and we watched excitedly as Arthur Numan starred for Holland in the 1998 World Cup. That summer was a blitz of news. We signed player after player, including Giovanni van Bronckhorst, Lionel Charbonnier, Andrei Kanchelskis, Rod Wallace and Gabriel Amato. We also signed Colin Hendry from Blackburn for £4 million, an outrageous fee for a 33-year-old, but when the whole outlay went north of £30 million it didn't seem that much. We had the money, otherwise we wouldn't be spending it. Right?

We started badly. We were to play Shelbourne in the UEFA Cup at Tranmere, and we found ourselves 3–0 down at half-time. At this point it was 'come back, Walter'. However, we recovered to win 5–3 before beating them 2–0 at Ibrox. This match saw one of the most embarrassing spectacles I have ever witnessed at Ibrox. The Shelbourne players contained a few Celtic supporters who would bless themselves constantly when taking corners, taunt the fans and then ended the match with a huddle. This, of course, was done to noise up the 'Gers fans. It failed because, of course, they were beneath us. We simply refused to get annoyed by a gang of irritating no-marks.

This was the start of the Scottish Premier League (SPL), a breakaway League of the top clubs, which was going to usher in an age of prosperity unseen before in our wee country. What it seemed to mean was a deal with Sky TV and squad numbers. The SPL was run by an unheralded man called Roger Mitchell, who bore a stunning resemblance to Walter the Softy from *The Beano*. What he brought to the table was never quite made clear, but everyone started spending money on players like there was no tomorrow. Motherwell were suddenly bringing in guys on huge wages, for example.

We played very well that season. Advocaat favoured a strict 4–4–2 formation. Rod Wallace had arrived without much fanfare but quickly won over the crows with his superb work rate and finishing. Advocaat had promoted a young midfielder called Barry Ferguson, whose older brother, Derek, had starred for us a decade before. Barry was elegant, tidy and a really gifted playmaker. Jorg Albertz was still battering in 30-yarders on an almost weekly basis. We had Dutchmen aplenty and they were all useful. The 7–0 away battering of St Johnstone and the 5–0 over a very decent Kilmarnock side showed exactly what this team was capable of. The football was great, the results were good and we had a real laugh following the team. The atmosphere at games was one of expectation and usually joy as the team ruthlessly destroyed whoever was put in our path.

I started to notice the papers a bit more as I got older. You could tell which journalist supported which team. I remember a match report by Ewing Grahame of the *Daily Record* after we had come from 2–0 down to beat Dundee 3–2 with a last-minute winner. Advocaat had, somewhat understandably, been a bit excited by this development. He had run from the dug-out to his players to celebrate before catching hold of himself and heading back to his chair. Grahame wrote that Advocaat had indulged in a 'grotesque' celebration. Grotesque? Had he got a can of spray-paint from the physio's bag and written 'DUNDEE CAN LICK MY BIG DUTCH BALLS' on the tunnel wall, I'd have had some sympathy. But running to his players for a cuddle then running back? There's hyperbole and then there's mere stupidity. This was certainly the latter.

Advocaat did rub people up the wrong way. He was gruff and he didn't have time for idiots. This became a bit of an issue because every week it was part of his job to be interviewed by Chic Young. Chic has a strange interview style, a sort of overarching obsequiousness that is designed to let the listener know that he is good friends with whoever he is interviewing. This falls down slightly when it is often made crystal clear by the interviewee that they'd rather blow their chairman than spend a night in Chic's company. Advocaat's withering impatience with Chic as he faced a barrage of probing questions – 'Are you happy with the result?' being a good example of the Paxman level of interrogation on offer from the Beeb's man with the mic – gave the impression that he was arrogant, but he'd earned that arrogance. He was just good at his job, and he knew it. He was single-minded, and he'd stop at nothing to win the title. Neil McCann was signed to help ensure this, and then Stefan Klos arrived from Dortmund. Both would go on to be fine servants for the club.

This was really the start of David Murray's ego running wild. We signed Daniel Prodan for £2 million, despite him being unfit. This was apparently to stop Spurs from buying him. He never kicked a ball for the club. The very expensive Hendry deal was clearly a move by the chairman, as it was obvious Advocaat didn't think much of him. I had always thought he was a bit like a 'lite' version of Richard Gough, and although the big man tried hard, he didn't do anything to shift that opinion. His spell with us was short and unhappy, an expensive mistake in what was becoming a catalogue of errors. Jonas Thern had been signed on a ludicrous wage in Smith's last season. He was, according to legend, all set to retire until his agent let him know about the silly money on offer in Glasgow. He barely played during his time in Glasgow but trousered a reported £4 million for

his trouble. Where was all this money coming from?

On the field though, we just got better. It became clear that Rangers could not be stopped on our march to the domestic treble. We beat St Johnstone in the League Cup Final then continued our onslaught in the League. The scene was set for 2 May 1999. Rangers had a chance to win the title at Celtic Park. That is its official name, of course. Many call it Parkhead. Rangers fans are remorselessly productive in coming up with names for it. There are several which reference other stadiums, such as the Stadio Delle Alkie, the Brendanbeau and the Big Jock Nou Camp (we'll come to that one later). Then there are simpler ones which simply go for the insulting; the Girodome, the Piggery, the Potato Bowl. The best I've heard them come up with for Ibrox is Castle Greyskull, which derives from the *He Man* cartoon. This is, one would think, a bit of an own-goal from the East End Massive, as Castle Greyskull is where the good guys came from. The baddies came from Snake Mountain. It's either an act of mass idiocy or a very honest appraisal of their role in Scottish football. This is very commendable

One particular match has a special place in football folklore. The game kicked off at 6.05 on a Sunday night, the time Sky TV insisted on. In reality, this meant people had the whole weekend to build up the tension and, of course, drink. It was a lovely, balmy day and Celtic were not best pleased at the prospect of us winning the League in their midden. There were a few major incidents in this match:

• Referee Hugh Dallas was struck by a coin thrown from the home end.
• A Celtic fan fell from the top tier of the stand. He was not badly injured.
• Several Celtic fans attempted to enter the field of play at various times to remonstrate the ref.
• Missiles rained down on Rangers players and match officials.
• £78 worth of loose change was found to have been thrown on to the pitch from the home support.

You may notice one common denominator in all of that – the complete lack of any disgraceful actions from the Rangers support. Yet, for some reason, this match has come to be known as the 'Old Firm Shame Game' instead of the 'Celtic' shame game. Let's just be absolutely clear on the 'appalling' scenes that day. It was nothing to do with us. We didn't do nothing, guv. So why is it always apportioned to both sets of fans?

It's the old mythology again. You couldn't possibly just have bad behaviour solely on the part of the 'Greatest Fans in the World'. We must have goaded them. But Rangers fans were not involved in any 'shame'. It was purely and simply the home support. Any attempt to suggest otherwise reeks of agenda. Not every Celtic supporter was badly behaved, nowhere near the majority, in fact. The vast majority of Celtic fans are perfectly normal human beings. But the bad behaviour that day came from the home support. That's where the finger of blame should be pointed.

We won 3–0 that day, absolutely destroying them thanks to a virtuoso performance from Neil McCann. The players celebrated the win at the end by performing a mock huddle in front of the Rangers fans. This was naughty. While there was justification for the one performed at the end of the nine in a row game – Celtic had done so in the Cup game and Rangers were merely reciprocating – this was done purely as a 'get it up ye' on a powderkeg day. I'd be lying if I said I didn't enjoy it, though. However, the great law of giving it out and taking it again meant that if Celtic wanted to take the piss out of us in victory in the future, we had no comeback. You can't lap up your team lording it over the opposition then squeal like Bonnie Langford when the opposition does the same to you. And given the way the next decade was to unfold, Celtic would have lots of opportunities to get revenge.

The game had long-lasting consequences for Scottish football. It was decreed that the Old Firm would never again meet in a match to decide the title. In every other country, the League tries to organise the fixtures to manipulate a situation like this; in Scotland, we go out of our way to avoid it. This is a police decision, however, and I'm not going to criticise it. I don't have to deal with the aftermath of a particularly fervid Old Firm match. It also sounded the death knell for games kicking off at 6.05 on a

Sunday night. This was not a bad thing. It was a phenomenally stupid kick-off time, as you spent all day waiting around with very little to do but booze. It suited Sky but no one else. Losing it was not a bad thing from the point of view of those who attended matches, but it made the game less attractive to Sky, which was to have a serious impact on the SPL down the line.

As if to make this whole thing even worse, the Old Firm were due to meet in the Scottish Cup Final to end the season. The match was to be held at the newly refurbished Hampden, which is something of a disappointing stadium. You are miles away from the pitch, there is a sterile feel to it and the wind still howls round the place. The authorities drummed it into both clubs – behave, or else. The SFA then, in their infinite wisdom, appointed Hugh Dallas to be the referee. Celtic fans howled about how unfair this was. Then again, the SFA could have appointed the Pope and some Celtic fans would still have been miffed about it. Dallas deserves enormous respect for taking the game. Given the crap he'd gone through during the previous match, he would have been well within his rights to tell the SFA where to stick their showpiece match. It also took enormous grapefruits to referee it fairly, which he did. We scored at the end of the first-half through Rod Wallace, who had been superb all year for us. Celtic came back at us at the end and had a penalty shout when Lorenzo chested a netbound shot from Tommy Johnson past the post. It would have been easy for Dallas to cave in and give the penalty, but he made the right call and we had won the treble again.

This perfect season was to get even better when, the very next day, Kilwinning Rangers won the Scottish Junior Cup for the first time in a century with a 1–0 win over Kelty Hearts at Firhill. The whole of the town seemed to be there from what I remember, which isn't much; I had been properly blootered the night before and it just seemed to keep going through the Sunday. Still, the hangover was worth it. We were the treble winners, and our little Ayrshire cousins were the best Junior team in the country. These were heady days indeed.

Then came Findlaygate. Donald Findlay QC was Rangers' vice-chairman and a bit of an eccentric character. He was famous for his pipe and whiskery beard, and he had been the light-relief to David Murray's relentless pursuit of success. He was a committed Rangers supporter, and he played well with the fans. At the celebration held at Ibrox when the team returned with the trophy, he was secretly filmed singing the Rangers song *The Billy Boys*, a controversial number which included the line 'we're up to our knees in Fenian blood'. The footage was sold to a newspaper and splashed all over the front pages. Findlay resigned in disgrace, immediately branded a bigot.

For me, this was the turning point in Rangers' relationship with the Scottish media. After this, it was open season. Rangers had shown that if you attacked them, they would roll over. Findlay was hung out to dry and the club allowed him to be so. You could argue the semantics of the song – I later did, badly – but it was a song sung by 50,000 Bears most matchdays. He had been singing it at a private party. Therefore, the accusation that he was guilty of causing offence is ludicrous. Who was likely to be offended by this at that party?

Now, Findlay was a bit arrogant and he had enemies in the press who enjoyed seeing him suffer. But he didn't deserve to have his professional reputation impugned over this. He had sung a football song at a football event. He should have apologised for any offence caused and moved on. That he didn't gave some people the idea – the correct idea – that it was open season on Rangers. And so it proved.

Advocaat ruled Scottish football at this point. He was the man. Everything he had touched had turned to gold. He was direct, sharp and hungry for success. Celtic had a chief executive at the time called Allan McDonald, who seemed caught up in the maelstrom that had engulfed Celtic since Fergus McCann left. He ordered a psychologist's report on Dallas' performance in the 'Old Firm Shame Game'. This pathetic episode in Scottish football history is often glossed over. McDonald's spurious excuse for doing this was that they wanted to learn a lesson from the match to prevent an occurrence of any similar scenes in the football. What he really wanted, of course, was to pander to the loony wing of the Celtic support. He should have at least been honest and said 'it wisnae oor fault, it was the bastard ref'.

One did wonder who he was to question anyone's mental state when he announced who Celtic were appointing to take on Advocaat next season: the Dream Team. Kenny Dalglish was appointed as director of football, a role that apparently meant playing lots of golf in Spain. It also meant overseeing the new head coach, one John Barnes. His first job in football management would be with one of the biggest clubs in a League he'd never played in. Laugh? I almost bought a round.

Celtic made a few signings, but I have to mention one in particular as a wonderful example of a Celtic tradition. They unveiled the signing of a promising Bulgarian midfielder called Stiliyan Petrov who, after a slow start, would go on to be a terrific player for them. He was 19 years old and from Sofia. At his press conference he announced he was excited to sign for Celtic as he had been a huge fan as a child, with Kenny Dalglish one of his heroes. You see, he had had a Celtic Subutteo team when he was younger. This is a popular Tim trick that helps feed the myth that they have millions of fans worldwide. Everyone, when they sign for them, tells of how they were reared by grandfathers with tales of how the Lisbon Lions won the European Cup. They speak of little else in downtown Montevideo. Petrov claimed that Dalglish had been one of his heroes growing up, but he'd have been seven – in Bulgaria – when Dalglish hung up his boots. Why do they make players do this? Their fans don't care if the guy was a fan or not, just if he is any good!

1999–2000 seemed to be a season that held great promise for us. We were miles better than anyone else in Scotland and we had signed a new striker called Michael Mols who hadn't, I believe, been a Rangers fan as a boy. Mols was the football equivalent of the artist starving in a garret. He was 29 and played for Utrecht, not one of Holland's most illustrious teams. Although he cost £4 million, the only team who were serious bidders for him apart from us was Sheffield Wednesday. But he was brilliant, absolutely incredible. He arrived and hit Scottish football like a hurricane. He was quick and exceptionally skilful. He had a turn which saw him receive the ball, jink one way and then pirouette off in the other direction at a pace that would make Speedy Gonzalez look like a fat rat. No matter how often he did it, defenders couldn't get their head round it. He played football as if he were a kid. He just radiated joy when he had a ball at his feet, and he was devastating in the last third. In his first match at Ibrox, he scored four against Motherwell (with no less than Andy Goram in goal). He followed that up with two against a very decent Hearts team at Tynecastle, always one of the most difficult away venues for Rangers. We couldn't quite believe just how good this boy was. How had he managed to get to 29 without being spotted?

We drew Parma in the Champions League qualifier. Scottish teams don't knock Serie A teams out of Europe. And they had some wonderful players – Hernan Crespo, Abel Balbo, Juan Sebastian Veron, Fabio Cannavaro and Ariel Ortega among them. The first leg at Ibrox was magical. Cannavaro was sent off after half-an-hour, which helped, and we scored through one of our unlikeliest players – Australian journeyman full-back Tony Vidmar. Rod Wallace added a second and, unbelievably, we held on to take a 2–0 lead over there. I still couldn't let myself believe that we would do it. I didn't want to feel the crushing disappointment of being so close to something magical just to watch it slip away. It's like getting Jennifer Aniston's bra off and then not being allowed to touch. You'd never get over it.

The second leg was incredible. An away goal would have put the tie to bed, but you need the ball for that and that was something we didn't see much of it that game. They battered us, but somehow, through a combination of superb defending, profligate finishing and sheer luck, we did it. It was an astonishing result, given the calibre of the side we were up against. The Champions League awaited us.

We had a tough Champions League draw that year. I say tough, my initial reaction rhymed with 'clucking bell'. Bayern Munich, Valencia and

PSV Eindhoven. The players we would be facing included Khan, Matthaus, Scholl, Basler, Kily Gonzalez, Cruz, Mendieta, Nilis and van Nistelrooy. You've got the guts of a cracking fives team there. The funny thing is that we really fancied ourselves. We had a good side and we knew it. The Scottish press made a howling arse of it before it started when Hugh Keevins labelled Valencia 'the Aberdeen of Spain'. This was a side that would reach the Final in this and the next season.. They beat us 2–0 in the Mestalla, but a blind man could see they were quality.

It looked an uphill battle from there, especially after a heartbreaking draw with Bayern at Ibrox. We were excellent against the Germans, who spent most of their time on the ground. Big Jorg gave us the lead and we were good for it. After yet another German dive in the last minute, the ref was conned and awarded a free-kick. And, of course, it was a free-kick that they equalised from, via a deflection. That was a severe kick in the stones, let me tell you. We now had one point from two games and a tricky tie in Eindhoven next. Advocaat appeared to go insane when he left out Jorg. Of course, after an injury, the big man came on and grabbed the winner, a superb result. It's not easy to win away in the Champions League. It started in 1992 and Celtic still haven't managed it. Really.

The next game was PSV again, this time at home, and again big Jorg was left out. It was starting to look personal between him and Dick. Ibrox was more excited than a teenager with the new Grattan catalogue. The place was just bouncing. The Dutch looked intimidated, and I don't blame them. We humped them 4–1 with Neil McCann scoring two. Looking good for qualification, we welcomed Valencia to Ibrox. They beat us 2–1, but there was no disgrace. They remain the second best side I have ever witnessed in the flesh. They were superb. They hunted for the balls in packs of three, always seemed to have a spare man and could spring from defence to attack in a second. We were a good side and we couldn't get near them.

So on to the Olympic Stadium in Munich. It was some place. My erstwhile Trust chum Stephen Smith remembers very little of it after a calamitous session on the ale. The Germans were so wonderfully stereotypically German that night, you could have been forgiven for thinking they were engaged in a parody of themselves. They dived. They fouled. The hassled the ref. They rolled around as if broken. They won a questionable penalty, which they scored. We hit the woodwork three times. Of course, having lost the Final the previous season to Manchester United in spectacular style they probably felt they were due a slice of luck.

Our luck completely ran out when Michael Mols leapt out of a tackle with Oliver Khan on the touchline and landed awkwardly. His knee crumpled under him and his face betrayed the seriousness of the injury. The grin was gone, and in it's place was a grimace. His knee was destroyed and was never the same again. As Advocaat so memorably put it, Mols was 'at war with his knee'.

Domestically, we were untouchable. Celtic were dire under John Barnes. He played a mad new 4–2–2–2 formation, which apparently AC Milan did, only not noticeably to anyone other than the Jamaican genius. We spanked them 4–2 at Ibrox in a match best remembered for Paul Lambert's cowardly assault on Jorg Albertz, which led to us getting a penalty and him getting new teeth. 'Cowardly assault' is probably a bit much; 'slipping and accidentally bringing down an opponent, who subsequently lands on your face knee-first' is probably more accurate. We then drew 1–1 at Parkhead when they should probably have won, but they weren't much cop, to be honest. We signed Billy Dodds from Dundee United as a stop-gap replacement for Mols. Opinion was divided on wee Billy; half the support thought he was an Aberdeen reject, while the other half thought he was a jug-eared Aberdeen reject. To be fair though, he was superb for the rest of that season. He banged them in and won over the crowd with his work rate and finishing ability. He was a very underrated player, but he always gave 100 per cent and he knew how to put the ball in the net.

We won the double that year, losing to Aberdeen in the League Cup but gaining revenge in the 2000 Scottish Cup Final. This Final was christened the 'Oranje Cup Final', as Rangers fans paid tribute to the Dutch contingent at Ibrox by turning Hampden into a riotous display of orange.

This was a bit naughty, of course, and had the more excitable members of the media spewing at the sectarian connotations of the colour orange. Only in Scotland could this be an issue. Aberdeen lost Jim Leighton to a broken jaw early on and had to put striker Robbie Winters in goal, making the game a bit of a farce. We won 4–0 and our hegemony in the domestic game was complete. It looked like we would rule the roost for the foreseeable future. However, Celtic's defeat to Inverness Caley Thistle in the Cup – Super Caley Go Ballistic, Celtic Are Atrocious – had been the death knell for the Barnes regime, and that summer they brought in Martin O'Neill to manage them. Football in Scotland was about to get very different, and Rangers fans were to embark on a tumultuous decade. We'd get to find out over the next decade both how good, and also how bad, it could be to be a Rangers fan.

10

Web Warrior

I got my first proper job in June 2000. I had left uni with a debt and a degree and no practical skills. In my considered opinion, anyone who wants to go to university or college should be forced to work a full-time job for a year so they realise just what a doddle education is. It was a massive culture shock for me – you mean I have to come here for eight hours? Every day? And I have 45 years of this ahead of me? You get less time for robbing a bank! Of course, the trick is to find something you enjoy doing, which I didn't realise at the time. As my hobbies at that age were drinking and masturbating, it was unlikely I was going to find anything that combined the two. As Tennents weren't going to employ me as a taster and Playboy didn't respond to my speculative letter requesting a job, I took a job in the recruitment industry, something I would often bitterly regret in the years to come.

It was boring and soul-destroying. It was populated by wankers who made estate agents look genuine. The women all wore these fake chiffon scarves and too much make-up. The men all had designer stubble like it was 1988 and talked about their golf swing. Very few of them cared about 'Nuggets' being reissued or who should play up front for us. I didn't fit in, and I needed an escape from the endless pointlessness of the whole thing. Thank God for the internet. For a naturally lazy bastard like me, it offered an alternative to hiding in the toilet and watching the clock. Internet access at work was in its infancy, and workplaces hadn't yet twigged the endless time-wasting potential it offered and subsequently put complicated security systems in place designed to stop anyone accessing anything interesting. It was generally just 'don't download porn'. That was cool. What good is porn when you are in an office with other people? I mean, it really only has the one purpose. And I'd imagine if you used it in the office for that purpose, you'd only get to do it once.

It was then that I noticed that *Follow Follow* now had a website, and on it was a forum. This was all still fairly new to me as I was a late adopter to internet technology. As far as I could see, anyone could post anything they liked about Rangers. As internet use has grown, forums have become far more organised and controlled. You still get a fair sprinkling of lunacy on the net, but there are rules and moderators and control. Back then, on this site in particular, it was like the Wild West. You didn't need to register or even log in. You just posted what you wanted to and on it went. And it was mental. Initially, there was a hard core of about 30 of us posting regularly. The themes were the same – football, Rangers, what Rangers meant to us, the media, society, how we fitted in, what our place was. This, of course, had been fairly common practice for net forums. Gangs of like-minded individuals shared what they thought and a little community formed.

This was liberating to a degree that I found exhilarating. From feeling like I was the only one who thought the way I thought about Rangers, there were suddenly a lot of people who felt the same way. I would spend a large part of my time posting on there, in among the dull tasks that comprised my working day. I found that I could get by in my job at about 40 per cent. No wonder the country is in the toilet. I felt for other people in the office who had to work at full pelt and were still only just about as successful as I was. My boss clocked it, though. He used to lecture me at least once a week on how I could achieve so much more if only I worked a bit harder. He said this as though it was a revelation, an idea that I hadn't had. I knew I could do better, I just didn't want to. I had all these new people to talk to. And it was growing every day. A revolutionary element of this online community was that you could be anyone you wanted. You could create a persona and free yourself of the things you didn't like about yourself. This obviously led to some difficulties and some severe disappointments, like a football equivalent of *Sleepless in Seattle*. You could be bewitched by someone's personality on the web and then meet up with them only to discover some total tool sitting across from you. One of my favourites, though, is a chap called Stuart. He's a moderator, and the only moderator I have ever known who is regularly banned himself. He's an anarcho-communist with a wicked sense of humour and a dislike of the establishment. When *Follow Follow* was in full-on royalist mode after the Queen mum's death, he had a gag up about her before the body was cold.

What was becoming increasingly clear to everyone except the media in Scotland was that fans had become bored of what was served up to them. It was the same old stuff day after day. The opportunity for supporter participation was limited. You had the phone-in shows, whose default setting was aggro. The punters thought the presenters were halfwits; the presenters thought the punters were barely sentient fools who should be grateful for what they got. The disdain that people in football had for the people who actually paid for football was staggering.

This is one of the strange things about our game in this country. Everyone hates it, absolutely hates it. Fans stumble from game to game annoyed to the point of homicide by referees, players, officials, ball boys, the design of the pitch, the cost of the pies, the temperature, the play and the half-time entertainment. Chairmen and club officials have the same underlying principle when it comes to giving the fans the satisfaction they crave: 'Ach, what are you lot moaning about now?' Everything is too much trouble for the people who run Scottish football. They launch initiatives or present services that could be categorised under the heading 'Will this do?'

114 They charge outrageous prices for sub-par facilities, awful food, terrible football and then they blame the fans for being 'too demanding' when they have the temerity to ask what they plan to do about it. They take over football clubs and then act as if they are being forced at gunpoint to do so. They cut corners, fail to plan for the future and then demand fulsome praise for any little thing they actually do manage to get right. Journalists, meanwhile, see themselves as a breed apart from all of this. Some see themselves as misunderstood sages, prophets without honour who have all the answers but are ignored. Others see themselves as a sort of Poundland Woodward and Bernstein, fearlessly dashing across war-torn Paisley to break the earth-shattering story that St Mirren have released six youth players. The final group just see the madness for what it is and do their job to the best of their ability. These guys don't get the telly gigs, but they don't get attacked in the street either. These are the ones fans actually like and would pay for their output, but editors generally operate the 'squeakiest wheel/most grease' policy and foist the idiots on us. It is beyond the understanding of most football chairmen and many journalists that the fans are actually a resource, something which could be used to make the game better.

This aspect is what has contributed most to the growth of football sites on the internet. On a club message board, the assumption is that you know what you are talking about unless you prove otherwise. This is the exact opposite from the starting point of club chairman and the media at large. They believe you are an irritant whose cash they need; therefore, you are to be stripped of said money as quickly as possible then sent away again. The fans had no voice and had no chance of getting one. What they did, at almost every club in Britain, was use the internet to develop one. Suddenly, they had a way of communicating directly and in areas outside the control of the people who sought to keep them apart. Suddenly, there was a strong community spirit and a place for those disenfranchised with modern football to go. It was intoxicating.

The early days on FF were just fun. The patter was superb, and it was no place for shrinking violets. If you couldn't hold your own, so to speak, you'd be mercilessly ridiculed for your ridiculous belief and you'd soon be sent packing, cybertear spilling down your pixilated cheek. Everything was up for debate, from signings, to seat allocations, from STV to Sky. One thing that was different in the early days was that Tims were allowed on. It seems fanciful now, but back then we went on their boards and they came on ours. There was a sort of détente in the air. These were heady days. Some of the abuse, though, you'd get jailed for now. But it was that or work. I can't believe that the Government didn't sense the effect that this phenomenon would have on UK productivity. I'm convinced our GNP dropped like a stone when Follow Follow.com was born.

Summer 2000 saw Dick go mental. Murray announced that we would sign a £10 million player. This seemed an odd thing to say. We weren't going to sign a good striker, or a top striker, but a £10 million striker. It's like deciding that you don't care which car you get so long as it costs £20,000. Advocaat ignored that temptation, however, and instead made two prize signings in Dutch internationals Fernando Ricksen and Bert Konterman. This boosted our Dutch colony to one larger than Suriname. He also brought in players like Paul Ritchie, Allan Johnston and Kenny Miller, then the hottest property in the Scottish game. Peter Lovenkrands arrived from Denmark. The joke was that Rangers weren't buying a £10 million player at all, rather 10 million £1 players.

Advocaat changed the shape from his usual 4–4–2 to a shaky looking 3–5–2. This was primarily to fit the two Dutchmen into his team. Konterman was an enigma. He's a legend at Feyenoord, but at Rangers he simply never looked like a footballer. He was timid, weak in the tackle, cumbersome and error-prone. Having had a solid back four for two years, it was tough to understand why Advocaat was messing around with it. Ricksen was just a disaster. This was never more clear than when he was taken apart in a 6–2 drubbing at Parkhead. He was subbed after 23 minutes for his own good. He looked as though he'd learned his positional sense from a drunk at closing time. Of course, in the grand conspiracy scheme, Celtic fans usually forget that their first goal that day was offside and that Rangers had a perfectly good goal disallowed at 3–1 just before half-time. Ricksen is a cult hero to some Rangers fans, but I couldn't stand him. He was an average player, had one good year – combined – in four seasons with us. And as for his hardman rep, don't make me laugh. Souness was a hard man. Kicking someone in front of the ref and getting sent off doesn't make you a hardman, it makes you a dolt. He cost us many times.

O'Neill's Celtic were different. They were pragmatic, physical and streetwise. Our season just fell apart. We lost at Aberdeen and at St Johnstone, and then we were thumped 3–0 at home by Kilmarnock. The players visibly couldn't arrest the slide.

Advocaat did what he always did. He spent. We bought Ronald de Boer from Barcelona for £4.5 million, an incredible signing. However, beset by injury, it took Ronnie a good year to get himself together. We were also close to a move for John Hartson, which we pulled out of due to a knee injury. He went on to prove that was a mistake when he hit over 100 goals for Celtic. He then made what is, and shall forever remain, the single biggest purchase in Scottish football history. He paid Chelsea £12 million for their Norwegian substitute Tore Andre Flo. Flo has become the byword for the largesse at Ibrox at that time, but he actually isn't the flop some make out. He scored 38 goals in 70 matches, but he simply didn't have the physical or mental attributes to be a pivotal part of any team. He'd been a perennial substitute at Chelsea for a reason. The £12 million tag weighed too heavily on him. For that money we expected the Second Coming. He could never live up to it.

This is when Murray's spendthrift ways started to alarm the support. We were about to post £30-odd million losses for that financial year – why were we spending £12 million on a player? Not only that, but we were absolutely devastated by injuries at that point. We had no fit defenders, except the seemingly unbreakable Bert, and that wasn't always a good thing. If we did have £12 million, why didn't we sign four or five players? The answer, of course, was ego. We'd said we were going to sign a £10 million striker and, by God, we were. Never mind that we didn't need him and couldn't afford him. Like a teenager with their first credit card, we were getting what we wanted and damn the consequences. Anyone who objected was called a moaner.

Murray's justification for this financial calamity was 'that he was chasing the dream'. If we did that, if we went out and ran up huge debts we could never hope to pay off on stuff we don't need and can't afford, and we used that justification, they'd put us in prison. The other mitigation Murray offered up was that 'no one complained at the time.' I don't even know where to begin with the stupidity of that one. It's the equivalent of a dad overspending at Christmas, and when the toys get taken back to the store turning to his crying kids and saying, 'You didn't complain at the time'. When you are the person who signs the cheques, you are the person wielding the power. You are also supposed to be responsible. Demonstrating absolutely no concern for the long-term health of the club is not responsible way to run the business.

The Champions League offered some solace with a 5–0 win over Sturm Graz, possibly the finest all-out attacking Champions League performance from a Rangers team. We then recorded a stunning 1–0 away win in Monaco. Advocaat demonstrated that he may have been stubborn and had made a few mistakes, but he was also a very good tactician. He deployed Turkish midfielder Tugay as a sweeper that night, and it was a masterstroke. The French had a very decent side but never really threatened to level the match. A 3–2 defeat in Turkey by Galatasaray was one of the strangest matches I have ever seen. In an atmosphere that was bordering on the lunatic, the Turks dominated and raced to a 3–0 lead. We were, as the cliché goes, lucky to have the nil. Then the players simply went for it, and were all over the Turks. We made it 3–2 and hit the post. This should have bred confidence, but the next match against them witnessed a strange selection, even by the standards of that season. We went 4–3–3 with Lovenkrands, who'd hardly played, starting on the left. It ended 0–0 and nothing happened. It was duller than an episode of *The One Show*. We then lost, embarrassingly and weakly, to Sturm in Graz. This had seen yet more fabulous spending. With Stefan Klos injured, it was felt none of our young goalkeepers could step up to the plate, so we spent £2 million on Jesper Christensen from Denmark. He played a handful of games and was sold on for £400,000. It all came down to the home match with Monaco. We were 2–1 up and heading through when an Amoruso mistake caused us to lose an equaliser. The big man had a tendency to try to play football in situations where it may have been more beneficial to just hoof the bloody thing. It was great when it came off, but when it didn't it generally led to a goal being conceded. Sure enough, Monaco pinched the ball off him in the last third and that was it. Out, nowhere in the League and all over the shop, the club turned on itself.

At the next match, some absolute idiot in the stand above where I sat in the Govan produced a banner that read 'AMO MUST GO'. I always wondered why he'd chose to go with the friendlier 'Amo' rather than 'Amoruso'. After all, a nickname indicates a fondness, which seemed at odds with a banner publicly calling for him to be shipped out of the club. I suspect it was because he was worried he'd struggle to spell 'Amoruso' correctly. I love Rangers supporters, and that night reminded me why; as soon as the banner was unfurled, there was collective rush to get it pulled down and the fella was taken aside for some harsh, but necessary, lessons in how to support his team properly. Advocaat was of the same mind as him, to be fair. He stripped Amoruso of the captaincy in a public humiliation and handed it to 22-year-old Barry Ferguson. It seemed Amo would be on his way out of Ibrox. The Rangers fans loved him, though, and simply wouldn't allow this to happen. They got right behind him and made it obvious they were still in love with the mad big Italian.

This is something I don't get about how Rangers fans are portrayed. If we are all howling bigots, then why did we adore our first-ever Catholic captain so much? How have the most popular players at Ibrox in the last decade been Roman Catholic? Did somebody forget to tell us? The truth is, as always, fairly prosaic. Rangers fans don't hate Catholics. The people who run the club have allowed themselves to be bullied into thinking that being a Protestant makes you, by definition, anti-Catholic. There is nothing wrong with being proud of what you are – for either side.

The highlight that season domestically was a 5–1 win over Celtic in November and that was it really. The press coverage of the two managers was in stark contrast. The press had fallen in love with O'Neill, and it was easy to understand why; he was a witty, intelligent man who was capable of great charm...when his team were winning. Advocaat was arrogant and aloof. He'd ran roughshod over the press for two years and they were itching to get back at him. The criticism of his team this season was savage. However, this was reflected by the grumbling from the stands. I have never seen a Rangers team just give up the way that team did. It was pathetic. There had been talk of divisions between the Dutch contingent and the rest of the players. Whatever it was, it was obvious the players had stopped playing for Advocaat. When he lambasted them in the press after yet another tame defeat to St Johnstone, it had no effect. That's when the game's up – when your players couldn't care less about anything you say, you've lost them.

Celtic won the treble that year, only the second in their existence. We could have no excuses, really, though some of our players did moan about injuries. Celtic picked up on this, and wore t-shirts with NO EXCUSES blazoned across them, which was ironic given Celtic's own history of excuse-making. This was when the media feeding-frenzy, threatened since Findlay's resignation, really came into effect. It was led by the *Herald*, Glasgow's premier newspaper, which had recently had a change of direction in terms of it's editorial policy. It was now populated by those of a more Celtic-minded persuasion, and they were free to pursue any agenda they wished to. I remember speaking to a venerable old broadcaster who worked for the *Herald* for years and asked why he was no longer with them. 'I didn't survive the cull' came the reply.

The *Herald* had two main sportswriters – Ewing Grahame and Graham Spiers. Grahame had written for the *Daily Record* and was actually quite a

good writer, though he was reported to have personal demons that plagued his career. Spiers was trying to create a persona for himself as the intelligent wing of the Scottish football press pack. He'd written a column for low-circulation broadsheet *Scotland on Sunday* for years, had done the odd telly thing and generally had not been noticed. He was known as one of David Murray's prime media lackeys. This was all about to change, however. Murray cast Graham aside around this time after Spiers had been somewhat indiscreet with a piece of info about the great man. This had caused Spiers to be denied access to the world of spoon-fed stories, free trips to Murray's Jersey mansion and expensive wines. Spiers had tried to get back into the good books with a series of arselicking articles but found Murray strangely unreceptive. Cast aside, Spiers turned his tongue Martin O'Neill-wards and began to stick the boot into Rangers at every opportunity, like a spurned lover cutting up his ex-partner's clothes in a fit of tear-stained regret. The bitterness just oozed from him.

Suddenly Rangers were a horrible club responsible for bigotry and their fans were lowlife scum who were a blot on the fabric of society. Let's get that in context. Rangers FC were responsible for bigotry in Scottish society. Not a part of it, but the reason for it. How, in the name of all that's logical can a football club manage that? A football club can be a symptom of society, but it cannot be a factor in forming it. It just isn't possible. Unless Rangers FC were issuing instruction sheets on how to burn down chapels efficiently, all they were doing were playing football matches, which people were attending. Spiers and Grahame wilfully misrepresented the culture of the supporters, made ludicrous assertions that went unchallenged and presented opinions as facts. All debate was cut off because there was as much chance of the *Herald* printing a letter from a Rangers fan as there was of me being selected to open for the Rolling Stones. It was a closed issue; we just were bigots. This wasn't a debate, it was an edict. Let the words ring out – Rangers are bigots. You should hate them. Things would get worse for us before they got better.

11

New Millennium, Nae Money

Summer 2001 was a period of massive adjustment for Rangers. We weren't the champions, and indeed had lost the League by a huge margin – 15 points, to be exact. Having won the League by 21 points the season previously, we'd allowed a massive 36-point swing inside 12 months. The fans expected an absolute blitz in the transfer market. It didn't happen. Claudio Caniggia, a legendary name but now in his late 30s, arrived from Dundee where he'd implausibly been starring. Russell Latapy arrived from Hibs, and the talented but perennially injured Christian Nerlinger arrived from Borussia Dortmund. This was not what we had grown used to, and we did not react well to it. Talk started to float round the ether that Rangers were in huge amounts of debt, but the consensus was that this could not possibly be true. Our owner was a multimillionaire, almost a billionaire. He had said he'd spend a tenner for every fiver Celtic spent to keep us at the top of the pile in Scotland. Those signings, like buses, would be along in a minute and in a group. We just had to give it some time.

We started the season reasonably well, playing some very decent football. Advocaat was, at heart, a purist. Schooled in the Dutch tradition, he liked his teams to knock the ball about and try to do so at pace. Celtic, however, were ruthlessly pragmatic. They just did not drop points. O'Neill's methodology as a manager is fairly simple. He gets massive players at the back and up front. He gets pacy players out wide. He gets a couple of guys who can knock in a terrific ball from a set-piece. His teams are then encouraged to win set-pieces in dangerous areas. This is not rocket science. I had to laugh when I heard Kevin Day criticising Aston Villa's players for going down too easily on *Match of the Day 2* on BBC2. This is what O'Neill's teams do. For Gabby Agbonlahor, read Henrik Larsson. For John Carew, read Chris Sutton. For Stiliyan Petrov, read, well, Stiliyan Petrov. It's not pretty to watch, like a sort of refined Wimbledon, but it is effective. We would drop points in places they simply wouldn't.

The signings did arrive, and they were top drawer. Michael Ball arrived from Everton for £6.5 million. At the time, he'd been tipped as a future England captain. Injuries would see to it that he never hit the heights his ability suggested he would. Shota Arveladze arrived from Ajax. I loved Shota right from the start. He banged them in wherever he went. Honestly, hit Wikipedia and find his stats. He was a fantastic goalscorer. Of course, being Rangers, we played him wide left for most of his career at Ibrox. Well you would, wouldn't you.

We were on a run of 11 wins when we came to play Celtic at Parkhead. Sadly, by this point, we'd developed a massive inferiority complex about playing them. Celtic thought they would win, and our players gave the impression that they felt that way too. We lost 2–1, and what really stung was the inevitability of the defeat. Advocaat had a screaming match with Ball on the touchline. The Tims roared with laughter. We sullenly went home and blamed the ref, the manager, the squad, the weather, the Vatican. It was just too painful.

Around this time, with desperation seeping in, the financial reality was starting to hit home. Rangers had amassed a lot of debt. A lot. It was around £50 million. It would peak at over £80 million. How could this have happened? The chairman had always gone on about how he'd put his own money in. So who did we owe it to? Him? This is the thing about David Murray. He gets away with a hell of a lot. If he put a lot of his own money in – a myth he loves to peddle – then how did this here debt thing get so out of control? Why were we borrowing these great fistfuls of cash from the bank? Whatever had happened, the bank was starting to get twitchy. The SPL had decided to negotiate their TV deal with Sky TV. In their infinite wisdom, they knocked back £48 million over four years. This would have ensured that the game was broadcast all over the UK from a reputable broadcaster with a proven track record who definitely had the cash. The SPL have since claimed that this was merely a negotiating tactic that they fully expected Sky to come back with an improved offer. It begs the fundamental question – why? Scottish football is, and was, pish. We watch it up here because we have to. It's not that exciting, the standard is fairly grim and there are only two teams anyone south of Hadrian's Wall has any minute interest in. Did they honestly expect Sky to come barrelling back in to the negotiating room on their knees with a huge offer? Sky have always been very up-front about their football coverage; it's the Premiership. Everything else is a hors d'ouevre to the main course. We were essentially asking them to pay huge sums of money for the snacks that they served their guests alongside drinks. Who was running the game up here? Did the selection process consist of running into a job centre and throwing a net over the first people they met?

This decision meant that the game in Scotland was screwed. Every club's budget was predicated on there always being oodles and oodles of cash to spend. Chairmen had apparently thought every day was going to be like the start of *Goodfellas*, with lots of places for us to go and fill our boots. Sadly, this was not the case. The BBC offered a far more modest two-year deal. The clubs decided that they would instead launch their own TV station. They couldn't run their own sport competently, but, yes, they were going to run a TV station. I bet you Rupert Murdoch was shitting himself. This station was going to be all-singing and all-dancing, and every football fan in the country would want it. But there were a few problems. I am a Rangers fan. I am interested in watching Rangers. I may occasionally watch other Scottish teams, but I will not pay money to watch them. Substitute the word 'Rangers' in the above statement for the name of any other SPL team and you have the feelings of almost every other fan. This was a monumentally stupid idea from a group of men who seemed to get up early in the morning to try to come up with new, more stupid plans than the last one. And, sadly, they often succeeded.

The Old Firm and Aberdeen voted against this disastrous course of action, and so the BBC deal it was. The diddy teams complained about it at the time. Had it happened, most of them would be bust today. They hadn't really grasped that money from an established broadcaster was guaranteed. If Sky said they were going to give you £48 million, then £48 million you were going to get. If company A comes in and says 'we will launch a TV company that will get loads of subscribers and pay you £100 million,' it is not guaranteed. Anybody can promise you any kind of magnificent figure. Anyone with a modicum of business sense looks at how they are going to fund it. The men running the SPL heard the bigger figure and simply went for it. Five-year-olds would have spotted the flaw. Instead, our clubs – who were budgeting for a golden age, where money flowed like Buckfast in a housing scheme – lurched from desperate situation to panic and back again. Motherwell went into administration. Dundee were well on the way to a £20 million debt on crowds of 4,000. Did no one running the game up here think where all this might be heading?

It was around this time of immense frustration and portentous black clouds hanging over the game that I started to write the odd piece for *Follow Follow*. I remember the excitement of seeing my first article appear on a matchday. I kind of expected that it would be held up in years to come as a sort of football equivalent of a Shakespeare play, a real cultural signifier and defining moment. Instead, even I can't remember what it was about. I was then invited to a meeting of the contributors in Annie Miller's salubrious city centre bluenose bar. I was almost overcome with nerves. I'd been reading these chaps' thoughts for a decade, after all. I had been introduced to the inner workings of the group by a fellow Ayrshire bluenose, Stevie Tyrie. Stevie is a far better Rangers fan than I'll ever be. He doesn't miss games. Ever. He could be undergoing a rather major heart attack and he'd still make it through the turnstile. His love of Rangers is matched only by his knowledge of the club. Stevie can tell you who came on as a sub in a League Cup tie with Alloa in 1961. He once asked me to compere a quiz he was running. I confidently strode up to the podium and started reading out the first question. 'There is a famous picture that hangs above the marble staircase at Ibrox, who is it' (cue everyone writing down 'Alan Morton', the man depicted in the portrait) by?' Not 'of', but 'by'. I'm pretty sure the artist's family didn't even know the answer to that one. It was only marginally less difficult than being asked to sum up Stephen Hawking's life work in 20 words. I thought the assembled quiztakers were going to lynch us. I took the only course of action available to me; I immediately and unequivocally put all the blame on Stevie.

Meeting Mark Dingwall, the editor of *Follow Follow*, was pretty nerve-wracking. These days I screen his calls, but back then it seemed like a big deal. Mark is a weird guy. He's simultaneously exceptionally cruel and exceptionally kind. He has the public persona (and profile) of a sort of Scottish Mussolini. Some people attribute pretty much every ill in Scottish society to his door. He gets accused of all sorts, most of which is patently bollocks. You can only take people as you find them, though, and I love the big guy. He's always been a good friend to me, and I'll tell you something, the Rangers support owe the man a vote of thanks. He got off his arse and organised a fanzine when no one else did. He spotted where all this was heading 10 years before anyone else did. He created a forum for people to get together. He encourages fans to take control of the club. Sure, he's the type of guy who laughs at funerals, but that's just his way. When Mark gets to the pearly gates and they ask him what he did for the Rangers, he's getting in, put it that way. He's my friend and I'm proud of that.

I was also fairly intimidated by meeting a writer by the name of the Gub, whose stuff I loved. He's my wee pal and I love him dearly, but good God, the man is hardcore. He makes me look like a season ticket holder at Parkhead sometimes. I had a seat next to him for a while. We used to joke that if some of the Celtic websites found out where, they'd launch a targeted missile towards us. His love of Rangers and all it stands for, however, is unsurpassed. He's not a big one for a friendly rivalry with the other side of the city, however. He once emailed an MSP with a polite query on why he was wasting parliamentary time with motions congratulating Celtic on their League title victory. The MSP in turn thanked him for his 'splendidly abusive' initial correspondence. I was proud of him.

I have a confession. I met my best friend in football due to *Follow Follow*. It embarrasses us both to this day, but Scot and I feel that it was more due to our love of music than football. Due to us this and the fact that we occasionally use moisturiser, we are the metrosexual boys of the Rangers community. The big man is Rangers daft and, like me, has high standards for the club. I like that; we should always strive to be the best. He's fiercely intelligent, the big man, one of the brightest guys I've ever known, and what frustrates him about Rangers is why they can't do the simple things well. I find myself agreeing with him most of the time. He's also great company to watch a game with, and we really do make each other laugh, even if no one else thinks we are funny. If you happen to get stuck next to us at a game, put your headphones on. Scot's a wonderful guy and we've had some amazing times watching Rangers.

Advocaat's time was up, and in January he moved aside into a director of football role. The choice to replace him was Alex McLeish. Big Eck had been a hero and mainstay in the great Aberdeen side of the 1980s. He had gone into management firstly at Motherwell – guiding them to a second-place finish – and then at Hibs, where he had taken them from the First Division and established them as one of the most attractive sides in the SPL. He had good credentials, but the fact that he was given the role was a little deflating **127** to the fans. Just three years ago, we'd been able to talk to (and had a good chance of attracting) some of the top names in Europe. Now we were being forced out of Harrods and into Debenhams for our shopping.

I liked Eck. He had dignity and a gravitas, and in his four and a half years at Ibrox he worked under some pretty difficult conditions. McLeish was there when the bill for the Advocaat years arrived, and he did as well as he could reasonably have been expected to do. What's more, he did it without complaint. He was a great ambassador for Rangers and he delivered trophies. In January 2002 we were miles behind Celtic, and McLeish found a club that had lost its swagger and couldn't see where the next trophy was coming from. His first big test came in a League Cup semi-final against Celtic. We won 2–1, the winner an extra-time wonder goal from the much maligned Konterman, who struck a magnificent 30 yarder into the top corner. Sweetly, he didn't really know how to celebrate it. We did though – Hampden was going tonto when that one went in. We beat Ayr United 4–0 in a fairly straightforward Final to record a trophy success for the first time in two years. We then had the rather intriguing prospect of an Old Firm Cup Final to end the season with.

There was confidence back in the support that day. We'd gone to Parkhead with a virtual reserve team and drawn 1–1, with Peter Lovenkrands scoring his third in three games against Celtic. It had been L'ubomir Moravcik's last game at Parkhead for Celtic that day, and when he was substituted he rose to take the acclaim of the Parkhead crowd. All you could hear was 8,000 Bears chanting 'Lubo's a gypsy.' It somewhat spoiled the moment. This is the type of comment which raises the ire of hacks. Is it offensive? Yes. Did it annoy the Celtic support? Oh, yes. You'll never remove that from the game. Why would you want to? They've sung some pretty horrible stuff at us over the years. You can either cry about it or accept it for what it is – a wind-up.

That Cup Final was just legendary. Celtic scored first through Hartson, but Lovenkrands equalised almost immediately. Celtic then reclaimed the lead through Bobo Balde. With half an hour to go, Barry Ferguson stepped up and commenced one of the best spells I have ever seen a player enjoy in a major match. He just refused to accept defeat. Rangers were winning that day; that was it in a nutshell. He crashed home a magnificent free-kick with 20 minutes left, then harried, prompted and passed Celtic into submission. They were dead on their feet and holding on for extra-time when Neil McCann teased a ball over in the last minute of time added on. Lovenkrands met it with a bullet header, we won 3–2 and all was right in the world. My Dad, perfectionist that he is, was a bit gutted it hadn't gone to extra-time, because we were giving them such a doing at the end he felt we'd have won 7–2 in extra-time. I'll take a last-minute winner any day. It actually worked out better for everyone, as the Celtic support seemed to collectively have an engagement to attend that evening. The ball hit the net as the clock read 92.16 and their end was empty by 92.19.

There was now serious panic in the air about a few things, however. This debt thing really wasn't going away. In fact, whispers had become voices, which had all but become shouts. This was added to the fact that the media was in competition to seemingly see who could make the most objectionable statement about how offensive Rangers fans were. Ewing Grahame in the *Herald* asserted that Rangers' new tangerine strip had played a part in the murder of a young Catholic in Northern Ireland. Graham Spiers asserted that when violence flared after Old Firm games, it was always Catholics who were murdered (something he was publicly corrected on by the Association of Chief Police Officers). Gerry McNee then stated that the Rangers song *The Bouncy* was a celebration of stamping on Catholic heads. This is a song with the words 'bouncy, bouncy, bouncy, bouncy nananananana'. The crowd then proceeds to bounce up and down while singing. It's not Noel Coward, but it is fun. You have to have a fairly diseased mind to find sectarian meaning in it.

To put this in context, Rangers' strip was a marketing ploy to cash in on the fact that many of the club's supporters are members of the Orange Order. It was a bit naughty, but that was all. It was no different to Celtic launching a strip based on the Irish tricolour, which they have several **129** times. That brought no comment. This piece of fabric led to deaths on the street. Back on planet Earth, please folks.

The Spiers and McNee ones are more insidious and actually a bit more dangerous. Grahame was just mental and hated Rangers. We could have donated our gate receipts to UNICEF and he'd have moaned about the font on the letter with the cheque. Spiers and McNee's claims had no factual basis. This was merely lying to get your point across, and it deflects from what you claim you want to do, such as ending bigotry. It would have been simple to find out the truth here. A phone call, one minute on the internet. But they chose not to. Why? It didn't fit with what they wanted to say. Spiers, McNee and their ilk have no interest in ending bigotry. It gives them something to write about. It lets them feel superior to other people and, best of all, let's them put the boot into Rangers. That's all it is about, in the final analysis.

Spiers is a weird one all right. I used to send him cheerfully abusive emails when I was younger. I remember the first time I was on radio with him. The BBC called and asked me if I would be okay to debate with Spiers by phone. I said I was on my way to meet someone in a restaurant and thus I'd be on a mobile, but they said it was fine and it would only be for five minutes. The call came and Graham was in the studio. I ended up on the phone for an hour, in sub-zero January conditions. He destroyed me, which wasn't difficult as hypothermia was starting to set in and I was in fear of my toes turning black and dropping off. Added to that, I was cut off whenever he spoke. It made debate somewhat one-sided, and I got monstered. You live and learn. The BBC were delighted with the feedback and asked me to do it again later that week. They hyped it all week on adverts on Radio Scotland.

The second time I said I'd only do it if I was in the studio too. I met him beforehand and he was extremely friendly, if somewhat remiss in personal hygiene standards. Then again, it was the end of the day, these things happen. Talking to him, it became clear. For all the linguistic flourishes, the air of West End frippery, the gauche aloofness, he simply wasn't very bright. He later accused me of being cocky, but I think it was more just certainty that I was dealing with a lesser mind, like playing scrabble with a monkey. I've met some media people whom I have instantly known were more intelligent than me – Tam Cowan and Stuart Cosgrove spring to mind – but I knew, even after the pasting I'd taken earlier in the week, that I was winning this one. Players sometimes say games are won in the tunnel; this one was won in the green room. I could say that I felt I had by far the best of the debate, but in more Scottish terms, I tore him a new arsehole. By the end he was trying to be pally with me as I patronised him into the middle of the next week. It was so cruel my dad actually gave me a row for it.

Spiers' main problem was that he'd fallen in with a bad crowd who used him as their useful idiot. He also liked the controversy it generated. If you ever had the misfortune to read Spiers' match reports, it was clear that he didn't actually like football and understood it even less. He'd get details wrong, like goal times, or stats about wins, or points, and then airily laugh it off when people pointed this out to him, as if it was unnecessary for a sports reporter to get facts right! When you think you are more important, as a reporter, than the story itself, it generally leads to the flatulent reportage that became his stock in trade. Spiers was convinced by those around him that this moral crusade he was on was for the greater good. It was a bit like tricking a child to do your bidding – simple, but definitely dodgy morally. The more attention he got, the more lurid the language and lies. It was a consistent message, which all but did for the *Herald's* circulation and made him continually less employable, to the point where he reaches fewer people now than the Entertainments section of the *Ardrossan and Saltcoats Advertiser*.

Having won the two trophies had saved the season somewhat but had glossed over the fact that Celtic had won the League at a canter. The new season saw us bring in Mikel Arteta from Barcelona, a wonderfully talented player who probably gained more from his time at Ibrox than he gave in terms of learning how to thrive in Britain. It was Everton who would eventually gain the full benefit of his time in Scotland. We had a decent team, though, with de Boer starting to play the way we knew he could, joined by Cannigia, Mols, Arveladze and Ferguson. Barry just bloomed that season. He was simply outstanding. No matter what happened in his future, anyone who had the pleasure of watching him that year was aware they were watching midfield masterclasses week-in week-out.

The biggest news, however, was that David Murray was standing down as chairman. This did not seem to be good news. The debt was being reported at £68 million, a truly astonishing sum of money. Given that the money in Scottish football is limited at the best of times, the worry was how on earth we were ever going to be able to trade out of it. Murray said that he felt the time was right to step back. It felt like he was leaving just as the brown stuff was about to smash into the spinning cooling device. He was replaced by John McClelland, a former IBM bigwig, who was given the mandate of steering the club through the forthcoming choppy waters. McClelland lacked the charisma of his predecessor, being essentially a colourless bureaucrat who had a track record in overseeing cuts in times of penury. It was tough to know how to feel about the change.

I've been accused of being anti-David Murray. That couldn't be further from the truth. Growing up when I did, Murray was as big a hero as any player (well, almost.) He was cool and determined, and he just radiated ambition. As a supporter, you trusted implicitly that he would deliver everything he said he would. He'd been the face of the good times. He was an enormous presence at the club. His departure at any time would have been a source of consternation, but given the whispers rattling around at the time it created more questions than answers. Rangers responded with what would become standard operating procedure over the next few years – nothing to see here, move along. This is all great news. Everyone at Ibrox is just peachy keen, and that debt thing? Just ignore it. Don't worry about it. Buy a strip. Buy a season ticket. Gie's yer money. A real fan would. Don't

ask questions, that's just bad form.

I've never understood why the club feels the fans can't be trusted with the information. After all, it always comes out anyway. Trying to keep information from spilling out of Ibrox is like trying to catch water with a net. It just can't be done. The club seems to feel it will prevent any panic by doing this, failing to realise that the contradictory sensation created by competing pieces of information simply leads to more supporter anxiety. People catastrophise, others simply plough on regardless. For some, the world is perpetually about to end, while for others a meteor could hit Ibrox and they'd still insist everything was fine and dandy. Either way, it leads to discord in the support, usually at a time when the club can ill afford it. However, the biggest problem Rangers would have for the rest of the decade – and still do to this day – is that they never seem to learn any lessons. When their hand gets burned in the fire, they still insist on walking right up and putting it straight back in again.

In terms of the football, the season started hilariously with Celtic knocked out of the Champions League in the qualifying stages by FC Basel. This led to the hilarious sight of Martin O'Neill throwing a tantrum and rolling about on the touchline in disappointment. If a Rangers manager ever does that, I will head the queue – which will be significant – heading down Edminston Drive demanding he immediately be sacked for conduct unbecoming of his office. What was all that about? It's like O'Neill's insistence on wearing football boots when he is on the touchline. Why? Is he going to come on if it's tight with 20 minutes left? You are the manager of a major football club and you are at your work. Wear a suit. As funny as this was, it would have unexpectedly far-reaching and potentially serious consequences when Celtic embarked on their amazing UEFA Cup run. But that was later. What was immediate was our own European humiliation, being dumped out of the UEFA Cup by the unheralded Viktoria Zizkov. In hindsight, it maybe wasn't the worst thing that could have happened to us. We had a talented squad, but not a big one. Throwing in added games could have had a deleterious effect on the title challenge. And we needed to challenge. We hadn't done so with any conviction for two years, Celtic seemingly having the League flag in their possession after about twenty minutes of the season kicking off. This year we promised to do a bit more.

We really were good to watch that year. We had several players capable of performing creatively, and a lot of goalscorers. Seven of our squad ended the season with more than 10 goals. Ferguson was the lynchpin. He'd added a free-kick proficiency to his game and, along with penalties, would end the year with more than 20 goals from midfield. His passing was crisp and sharp, and his leadership inspirational. He linked fantastically with de Boer and Arteta and we rolled on towards, unbelievably, yet another treble. The first leg of this was secured with a 2–1 win over Celtic in the League Cup Final. Lovenkrands and Cannigia put us 2–0 up, before Larsson pulled one back. With Celtic chasing hard for an equaliser, Bobo Balde landed on Chris Sutton and broke his arm. Of course, as football pundits tell you, you never want to see any professional footballer suffer a serious injury, but it *was* Chris Sutton. And it was his own player who did it. Celtic were then awarded a penalty in the last minute. Where's the bloody conspiracy when you need it? Luckily, John Hartson very sportingly saved us all the pain of extra-time by lashing his penalty closer to the corner-flag than the goal. Some Celtic fans at work suggested that he had actually done this to spare Celtic from extra-time, as they had so many big games coming up and wanted to conserve their energy. Then, just to make a great day both even greater and intrinsically more funny, Neil Lennon was sent off.

Why do Rangers fans hate Neil Lennon? The media – and Celtic FC – will tell you that it is because he is an Irish Catholic. This is nonsense. If it were the case, then Anton Rogan would have been the poster boy for the Rangers fans to throw darts at. I can't recall Darren O'Dea taking much abuse, either. Neil Lennon gets it because he is an irritant. He is Celtic through-and-through, which Rangers fans naturally don't like. He played football with a scowl on his face and he was annoying. He was the definition of the phrase 'a wee shite'. Ricksen was the Rangers equivalent, yet you never heard it being assigned to the fact that he was a Dutch Protestant. He got it because the way he played football made him a target for abuse. Similarly, Lennon got it because he was very vocally the representation of Celtic on the field. He was also – and this is key – very easy to wind up. You could get to him. Supporters note this. There was no point targeting Larsson because he'd ignore it, and likely score against you just to make you feel even more like a clown for starting on him in the first place. Not Lennon though. Some games, he couldn't even watch the match for sparring with the crowd at Ibrox. He infamously spat on a Rangers scarf thrown at him at Ibrox, and was clearly seen calling the crowd 'Orange Bastards'. This, as you might imagine, made him a bit unpopular with the home support.

This is where the religious make-up of the whole Rangers/Celtic thing falls down slightly. You get bigots in both supports. Out of a predominantly working-class support who number at least 110,000 match-going supporters, you will get some who are bigots. It's a cross-section of society after all. But the press assigns everyone into the 'bigot' camp with the burden of proof being on the supporters themselves to lift themselves out of it.

This is the great media lie of the Old Firm, that Glasgow resembles Belfast c.1974. It really doesn't. Protestants and Catholics work, live and hang about together. I don't know any Rangers or Celtic fan who doesn't have a friend from the other camp. They may slag each other off, but it's up to them to deem what they find acceptable, not the Scottish press and Government. I was married to a Catholic girl. We fell out about a lot of things, but it was not the pressing issue of the Catholic Church's insistence on the indivisible oneness of the Holy trinity or Martin Luther's nailed protests to the door that started those arguments. My friend Liam – don't be fooled by the name, he's a Tim – gives me it tight when Rangers are underperforming. I, in turn, roundly abuse him when the hoops are playing like shite. It's just banter. (By the way, it was Liam who said it was okay to use the term 'Tim' in the book, so if anyone finds it offensive, blame him.)

Celtic's European run was starting to get a bit worrying. They knocked out Blackburn and Stuttgart. This was a bit concerning, but it still seemed plausible they'd be on their bike soon. They then beat Liverpool. They became unbearable as the dire reality started to dawn on us – they could actually win the bloody thing. This was a prospect too horrid for your average Bear to even consider – real cold sweat in the middle of the night stuff. They were bad enough at the best of times, but a European trophy win? These days? Oh, dear Lord, no.

We had reached the Scottish Cup Final and were going strong at the top of the table, but despite another humiliating Scottish Cup defeat to Inverness – once is careless, twice is a beamer, as Oscar Wilde might have said if he was from Govan – Celtic were still on for the League and UEFA Cup double. They scabbed past Boavista in the semi-final. Hell is a Glasgow stuffed with smug Tims.

The reaction was one of sheer, undiluted joy from the media. Congratulations and good luck messages were announced in parliament, both the kiddy one in Edinburgh and the real one in England. Plans were made for an epic invasion of Seville. The streets of Glasgow would be empty that week, we were told, as thousands of Celtic fans would descend on the Spanish city. This was wonderful news for Glasgow store detectives, of course, but still intensely worrying for the rest of us. I thought they'd do it, purely and simply to annoy me. They didn't. Porto, under the guidance of the 'Special One', beat them 3–2. According to Celtic and their media cheerleaders, this was because of a shocking display of diving from the Portuguese team. It wasn't, of course, but that's Celtic; always cheated, never defeated since 1888. You think they'd be used to it by now. They booed the Portuguese as they collected their trophy

Celtic, magnificently, took 58,000 fans to Seville, an incredible achievement. That wasn't enough though, so the figure was raised to 80,000 in the press, which has become the official Scottish figure. I called it 'the Seville Calculator' on Real Radio once; you put a figure in and it suddenly multiplies for no good reason. I took my figure, by the way, from the UEFA and Seville police estimate, which put it at anything between 56,000 and 58,000. Celtic fans then immediately launched a web campaign encouraging other fans to email UEFA and demand an award for their remarkable behaviour.

We had, of course, decided to make it interesting in the League race. We drew 2–2 in a match at Dundee, in which Barry Ferguson missed two penalties. It shook him up so much he gave up penalty duty. The Old Firm just could not be separated going into the last game of the season. We were at home to Dunfermline. They were away to Kilmarnock. This made us slight favourites, as we always beat Dunfermline at Ibrox. But then again, Celtic don't come a cropper at Rugby Park all that often, so there wasn't much in it. Both teams were level on points. The plan was simple – go out and score more than they did. Easy.

The tension at Ibrox that day was exquisite. There was fear, but it was locked in a losing struggle with excitement. We scored early on, and what was most pleasing as raucous bellowing gave way to sheer frenzy was that the team grabbed the ball and hared back to the halfway line for kick-off. It shows intent, and while the seven seconds saved doesn't really mean a whole hill of beans in terms of the actual match, it gees up the fans. It says 'no time for celebration from us; we're all business'. I was so confident that we'd win that I wasn't wearing any colours that day, bar a scarf. I was already planning the celebration; therefore, I resembled an extra from Goodfellas, dressed in a long leather coat and shades. The downside, of course, was that the coat was just about all of the skin from a decent size cow and was extremely heavy. And it was May. And scorching. And tense. Ironic then, that in an effort to look cool, I looked like Dawn French after a press-up, such was the sweat.

Dunfermline, Fife bastards, then equalised. This was not in the script. However, we began to dominate and reached half-time 3–1 up. Celtic were also winning, but at this stage we were champions. There was a long way to go, though. I got a coffee. Just what I needed. Caffeine and more heat. I had now sweated more in one 45-minute spell than Alexei Mikhailichenko did in his entire Ibrox career. Celtic scored again. We scored again.

Celtic then got a penalty. Ibrox went silent and focused on sending bad vibes down the coast. It must have worked because Alan Thompson ballooned it over the bar. We raced into a 5–1 lead. They were 4–0 up with a minute to go. We were ahead on goals scored, not goal difference. If they scored one more, they would win the League. You could now swim in the immediate area surrounding my upper torso. I resembled a sweaty Tigger. The wee guy behind me gave me a toot from his hip flask to calm me down. Unless it contained liquid opium, it was unlikely to have that effect.

And then, in the 91st minute, we got a penalty. But Barry was off penalty duty, so who would take it? Step up Arteta. 50,000 people held their breath. The air just seemed to stop dead. There was silence. He stepped up and scored! As the place erupted, it was obvious that we had done it. We had won the League title, our record 50th League title. At the time, it gave us a 50–38 lead over Celtic (a Celtic fan of my acquaintance claimed this was due to our earlier formation, when in fact the first League was not contested till 1890).

The fall-out from this was just superb. Chris Sutton immediately claimed Dunfermline had lain down to us. That's the Celtic mindset in full lunatic effect. They win 4–0 – superb performance, well done lads, really professional. We win 6–1 – the other team must have cheated. Neil Lennon lambasted the Kilmarnock goalkeeper, Gordon Marshall, an ex-Celt, for not allowing Celtic to score more. Celtic fans went on the rampage in Kilmarnock, and I know this for a fact because my friend Chris, a Kilmarnock fan who despises both halves of the Old Firm, was at the game and told me so. You would not have read about it in the papers. They attack opposition fans – unworthy of comment. We sing a song in an empty stadium in Spain – the front page of the *Sunday Mail*. And we're paranoid, apparently.

The walk into town from Ibrox that day was amazing. Scot and I were surrounded by thousands of ecstatic bluenoses, and the joy was only multiplied by the sheer horror on the faces of our friends from across the city. Little did we know that this was merely a precursor of a far more seismic psychological destruction two years later. We did see a guy in a Celtic top in tears at the bottom of Oswald Street, clutching a bottle of vodka disconsolately. Our hearts went out to him.

We topped the season off with a 1–0 win over Dundee in the Scottish Cup Final. It was a non-event as a game, really, with Dundee the better side, but we got the job done. The winner was scored, fittingly, by Lorenzo Amoruso in his last game for the club. The big man shed a tear at the end of it, and was mocked on the TV by Graham Spiers for doing so. I wondered if Spiers shed a tear when he left the *Herald* after a few years employment, then I realised that I was being really unfair to compare the two situations. They were totally different – Amo was liked where he worked. They did both end up at smaller organisations earning less, right enough.

At the end of the season there was a strange atmosphere. Both sets of fans claimed that they wouldn't have swapped their experiences that season for anything else. We had the treble; they had nothing, but they did have the memories from a great run. I was jealous, as I didn't think I'd ever see my team in a European Final. I wished it had been us, and was grateful for the treble to offset that. It gave us a chance to move forward as winners. Little did we know it was the end of a good team and the start of some serious belt-tightening.

12

Helicopter Sunday

Rangers financial plight was obvious to all by 2003 and was made even more so by the ferocious firesale the club embarked upon. By summer's end, Ferguson, Amoruso, Numan, Cannigia and McCann had all departed for pastures new. Ferguson's departure hurt. He had been the man the season before. He had been the captain, and a bloody good one at that. He helped us into the Champions League before departing for Blackburn, not exactly a step up. Many fans felt he'd let them down. I could see he wanted to better himself by playing in a tougher League, but Blackburn? He also looked to be utterly fed up about a week after he arrived there. No offence to Blackburn, but it's not exactly a worldwide name in a football sense.

Given the black clouds hanging over the club, there had been talk of forming a Supporters' Trust. The concept of a Supporters' Trust was one that emerged in the late 1990s, as several clubs saw themselves being run into the ground by uncaring and/or incompetent owners. Fans would then have no option but to try to step in when the game was almost up and the club was in a near-irredeemable position. The Trust idea was Government-backed and theoretically allowed fans to improve their stakeholding in clubs and have a bigger say on how they are run.

Supporters Direct is the body which helps Supporters' Trusts. Their website states their role as 'providing advice to trusts on how to organise and acquire a collective shareholding in their clubs on a not-for-profit basis for reinvestment'. This, in turn, helps to secure greater level of accountability and deliver democratic representation within football clubs and within the game's governing structures. They deliver advice and guidance on leadership and financial accountability to their members and to ensure the Trusts play a valued and responsible role in the running of their clubs, improving communication and building a better relationship with the local community.

Sounds fairly honourable, right? And indeed it is. Each club is legally allowed one Supporters' Trust. At Rangers, the idea was simple; everyone joining would be given one share, which would then be used to help the fans build up a greater shareholding in the club and theoretically take control of a significant enough shareholding to be more heavily involved in the long-term decision-making at the club. The Trust does not want to pick players or managers. They are not there to decide on day-to-day football matters but to improve the relationship between fans and the club, and to prevent the dire financial messes we have sadly witnessed at so many British clubs over the last decade or so.

The Rangers Supporters' Trust's stated aim is very straightforward – 'The Rangers Supporters' Trust has one simple aim: to encourage and facilitate supporters of Rangers FC to buy and hold shares in the club in order to influence future decisions. The future of Rangers must be in the hands of people who care about the club rather than just seeing it as a financial investment. The long term aim of The Rangers Supporters' Trust is to deliver ownership of the club to its loyal supporters.' This is revolutionary talk in British football. Club owners see it as an attack on their competence. It isn't, per se, but given that Rangers were in massive debt with seemingly no way to get out of it, then it's fair to say that the Trust was formed due to supporter concern. But then again, Rangers fans conservatively put £25 million into the club each year through ticket and merchandise sales. They are not conventional 'customers' in that they have no intention of leaving the club to follow another team. There is no brand war here. The club trades on that loyalty. Adverts for match tickets hint at 'being part of the club'. This is a deliberate ploy to push the fans' buttons to make them feel they should be contributing to the club, and that's fair enough. In return, however, the fans want a say in what happens to that money. The 20th-century model of one rich man making all the decisions has been shown to be unsustainable in the 21st century. Owners may disagree, but the muddle the British game is in shows that to have been clearly demonstrated. Simply put, it was the old model of ownership which led the game to the brink of financial meltdown; therefore, it is time to look at new, innovative methods. And the big thing about supporter ownership is this; managers, players, chairmen and chief executives leave, but supporters are there for life.

To give you an idea of the contempt Rangers hold their fans in at times, let's do a wee pop quiz on what Rangers FC's reaction was to the news that Rangers were about to get their own Trust. Was it:

a) thinking 'we don't know much about them, but they are fans who obviously care about the club, so let's get together with them and see if they have any ideas that might help the club through this difficult time' or

b) to bad-mouth the idea before they'd heard anything about it, attempt to set up their own Trust to stymie the independent one, and when that failed set up a puppet 'fans' organisation', which they gave £30,000 a year they could control?

If you said a), congratulations on getting this far through the book despite being a halfwit. If you said b), step up and claim your prize.

Why do Rangers fear fans' input so much? I genuinely don't know. To me, it seems common sense to utilise the ideas and input of a self-organised customer focus group, which devotes time and energy and doesn't ask anything in return other than a better club. I think it speaks of an unbelievably reductive arrogance that no one at the top thought to do that. Their feelings about it were made clear at the AGM that year when the board was asked about the £67 million debt and about inviting fans input. 'I tell you what,' thundered John McClelland, doing a convincing impression of a tubby buffoon, 'if the fans ran the club the debt would be £167 million!' There you go, direct from the chairman. Puppet chairman he may have been, but chairman nonetheless. You lot are idiots. How dare you question us. This may be a calamitous situation, but it's a damn sight better than what you bottom-feeding inbreds would have managed. Frankly, it's amazing you don't accidentally set fire to Ibrox every second week. Gie's money.

It's hard to get angry at McClelland. He was dealt a shit hand and did nothing with it. He gave the impression of being slightly dim, and I always felt so long as he had a cup of tea and a biscuit he was happy enough. He waddled into press conferences demanding the respect that his high office brought him, unable to grasp that while the man can make a position, it doesn't automatically work the other way round. You could elect me president of Europe and I'd still be a fanny. Similarly, being chairman of Glasgow Rangers didn't make McClelland any thinner, brighter or more efficient. It just got him a large club blazer and a tie.

The first meeting of the Trust had taken place at Partick Burgh Halls. I attended and even asked a question about how Northern Irish fans were treated by the club, but didn't join. I saw myself as the classic liberal, wanting to carefully evaluate the pros and cons before committing to anything. Mark, Stevie and Scot were all elected to the inaugural board, however, so I was pretty aware of how it was developing. I didn't really see it as my bag, though. Protests and organised campaigns? That sort of thing was for the other lot.

This is one of the strange things about the Rangers support. We really do tug the forelock to the rich man in the big hoose. There is a large percentage of our support that sees any criticism of those in charge of the club as heresy. Having spent a large part of the last five years living under threat of being burned as a witch, I can vouch for this. This attitude is encouraged, even fostered, by those at the top of the club because it means their more awful decisions and basic incompetence is rarely analysed. But I understand it. I was a great believer in the idea that things would always get better. It's far more comforting to assume that it is only a temporary blip and that someone else will sort it out for us at some unspecified point in the future. The constant promise of jam tomorrow.

Eck had been forced to shop around in the bargain bins and had come back with a motley crew including ex-Middlesbrough midfielder Emerson, former Southampton and Blackburn striker Egil Ostenstad and Henning Berg, formerly of Manchester United. Only Berg really did anything of note. Emerson started brightly but then faded. He had disappointed me instantly due to having cut off his elaborate 1980s-style Soul Glo wet-look perm. Egil though – holy shit. This guy was abysmal in a way that looked like he'd been summoned from the stands, infected with the Ebola virus and then told to try to run it off as part of some mad scientific experiment. Everything looked a hassle to him. He barely moved. I was privileged to see his only goals for the club in a League Cup tie at Ibrox. They were to prove as unique as a unicorn roller-skating. I've actually broke out in a sweat typing this as his 'performances' came back to mind.

This wasn't Eck's fault. He'd been told to sell players and bring in cheaper ones. He'd done so. He didn't have much of a scouting system in place so had to rely on agents' recommendations. It was no surprise he would go for players who he knew by reputation. The problem was he was signing them on what they had been, not what they were. Managers do this a lot. Even Sir Alex bought Laurent Blanc in because he'd coveted him for a decade. Sadly, the guy he thought he was getting was a player in his memory; the real deal was way past his prime. Eck's most notable example of this was Nuno Capucho, the Portuguese international whom he remembered destroying O'Neill's Celtic at Porto a few seasons before. But that winger was gone. The guy we got was simply not up to it. Sadly, that's why he was prepared to come to Scotland in the first place. If he'd still been any good, he wouldn't have signed on to come to the SPL. Nuno, however, remains a legend for getting hammered in a nightclub, getting his willy out and waving it at passing ladies while shouting 'jiggy jiggy'. I don't give a damn whether or not you rated him as a player, that's behaviour which makes me proud to be a man. Being a footballer, of course, he wasn't arrested. Only footballers can wave their willies at women, and even then only successful ones.

So from the highs of a treble to the lows of sheer incompetence. We were, to be frank, mince. Nothing seemed to go right. Players got injured, we played poorly, teams started beating us easily and the League was over by Christmas. We signed Frank de Boer in January to come and play for a few months before heading to Qatar with his brother. He was a terrific defender, but signing him was akin to trying to repaint the Sistine Chapel with two tins of emulsion. The season just got worse and worse, limping along like a wounded deer in need of execution. There were some humiliating defeats to Celtic at the end of the season, and it was gone.

The Champions League offered much – again – but delivered little. You may have noticed a pattern emerging. We drew Manchester United. It threatened to be wildly exciting, and the first match at Ibrox was indeed. The noise level was phenomenal. United defender Gary Neville said it better than I could: 'This was the loudest atmosphere that I have known, compared to any English ground away from home. There have been certain nights at Old Trafford in European games – the ones against Juventus comes to mind – when the atmosphere was incredible. But this was definitely up there with the best. It was fantastic. When we came out at the start I was looking around me and I saw people in the directors' box jumping up singing and I was wondering what was happening. It is not usually like that.' United scored after five minutes through Phil Neville and, although we ran them close and should have equalised when Lovenkrands went for glory rather than sliding Shota in for an open goal, it was a creditable performance. The second game wasn't. They beat us

3–0, with Diego Forlan hitting two. We knew before everyone else that he was good. United, I have no doubts, went easy on us. Had they wanted to hit six or seven, they could have. Our fans that night were superb, singing defiantly from first to last. This upset some people.

Our old friend Graham Spiers went ballistic at us the next day in the *Herald*. Some descriptions taken from his piece: 'rancid chanting', 'total embarrassment', 'poisonous atmosphere', 'savages', 'desecration', 'cavemen', 'wholesale yobbishness' and his party-piece 'almost to a man'. You may think it was like a National Front meeting in there. It wasn't. Some fans sang some songs, none of which drew the ire of the 67,000 Manchester United supporters, the television commentators or the thousand or so police officers on duty.

Spiers' diatribes were becoming weekly events. The point of this was never made clear. He attended a fans' meeting at Ibrox once where, hilariously, he asked for security. He told fibs, talked bollocks and avoided questions. He went on a rant about how his 'mission' was to rid Scottish football of sectarianism. His immediate resignation would have gone a fair way towards that. The light of control went out in his eyes when he said this, and instead there was the unmistakable glow of madness. 'Oh Christ,' I remember thinking, 'is there anything more dangerous than a simpleton with a mission?' I asked him if he thought making the audience he was trying to reach hate him may prevent his message getting through. He stammered for a bit then said that the support had to be told the truth. I asked him again what he saw changing. He admitted nothing. So what was the point, I asked again? Here he was waxing poisonously about a subject he wasn't intelligent enough to grasp the complexities of. It was like listening to one of those obnoxious sixth-formers prattling on about the Middle East because they saw Newsnight once.

The financial situation had now made us a complete laughing stock. Fans had taken to waving money at us at away games. This was especially ironic at clubs who were equally as destitute as we were, but it's football. You rip the piss when the opportunity arises. Suddenly, news of a big announcement about Rangers started leaking out of Ibrox. Nobody knew what it was, but it promised to be big. The next thing was a horrified Trust in the papers declaring that Ibrox should never, ever be sold and calling on the club to quash rumours of an impending sale. There was silence from the club for a few days, during which time everything went utterly tonto. The fans were outraged, absolutely appalled that anyone could think of selling Ibrox. The fans had paid for that stadium through the Rangers Pools drive of the 1970s and 1980s (they did not, as Murray infamously put it during one of his unguarded moments, 'get it for free') and saw it as the lasting tribute to our absent friends. After a curiously long silence, the club said it had no intention of selling Ibrox.

To this day, they haven't. Stadium Investment Group (SIG) was a business operated by a close business associate of Murray's called Gavin Masterton. They specialised in the purchase and redevelopment of football stadia. They had been responsible for developing offices at Livingston FC's Almondvale stadium, which no business had wanted and had subsequently driven the club to near-extinction. SIG ceased to exist not long after the Rangers announcement, with sources close to them saying that a huge deal they had banked on had unexpectedly failed to materialise. I was just glad the Trust had got the club to issue such a cast-iron guarantee. Indeed, I was so impressed by this development that I finally joined, becoming member number 1300.

I was also stunned at the vitriol that was poured on Colin Glass, the Trust chairman. In several newspapers he was at best labelled a troublemaker and at worse had his sanity and integrity viciously decimated. Why were these so-called neutral journalists so quick to make up their minds? Especially without talking to him first? All I can say is that I was awe-stuck by how dignified Colin remained during this period. It seems you don't need to be a rich man to have class, and that money can't buy you basic decency.

Finally, the season ended. The de Boers left after a faintly embarrassing presentation before our last match of the season against Hearts, which, in **147** keeping with the year, we lost. I said to Scot that I believed the departure of Ronald de Boer was the last time we'd see a genuine world-class talent plying his trade at Rangers. Sadly, six years later, I believe I was right. It wasn't simply a player leaving that day; it was an era. The days of wild financial largesse, of reckless gambling, of ego-driven non-sustainable spending were gone.

The club realised we couldn't have another year like that. We'd redefined 'pish'. With this in mind we brought in some new players, many of whom were to prove very decent indeed. Dado Prso arrived from Monaco on a Bosman. Prso had played at Ibrox when Advocaat was in charge and had apparently been so blown away by the atmosphere that he had wanted to play for the club ever since. He had scored four goals in one Champions League match against Deportivo La Coruna the previous season, so his arrival was very exciting. Given the whole-hearted way he played, we soon fell in love with him. Alongside him was Ignacio Novo, better known as Nacho. He cost £400,000 from Dundee, and it was the best £400,000 Rangers have ever spent. I've seen Nacho described as a cult hero at Ibrox by the press. This is another example of football journalists not understanding what the words they use mean. A cult hero is someone who isn't loved by the masses, but rather by a small group within the support. He wasn't – everyone loved him. He was all about energy, commitment and drive, and he loved the Rangers. Not in a badge-kissing, showy way, but in a visceral fashion that you could see every time he took to the field. And he seemed to have about the same opinion of Celtic as we all did. The Celtic fans despised him for one simple reason: he knocked them back. His agent famously made him travel to meet with Martin O'Neill for talks. These lasted five minutes, with Nacho informing the Leaping Leprechaun that he was signing for the Teddy Bears. Nice one, Nach. The Bhoys never forgave him for it. We, of course, never forgot it either.

At the back was Marvin Andrews. Big Marv was as famed for his deeply held religious beliefs as he was for his agricultural defending style. He'd arrived on a free from Livingston to many raised eyebrows but would have a good year. Marvin's religion was one of love, joy and kindness to others. It was mercilessly mocked by the press. The same press, of course, who sent reporters into the Rangers End hoping to hear dirty words about the Pope. Irony – to some people it's just too much to grasp.

My favourite exponent of this was Elaine C. Smith, the dismal Scottish actress who was given a column in the *Sunday Mail* to proclaim how great she was, how she wanted independence for Scotland, and her love for Celtic. She got stuck into Marvin until she received a flood of letters complaining. She said we should all be a wee bit less uptight about religion. This was coming from someone who practically wanted people birched for daring to suggest that maybe her own beliefs were not to everyone's likings. She was not a great one for practising what she preached.

Next to Marv was Jean-Alain Boumsong, then one of football's hottest free agents. No one could figure out how we'd managed to lure him from Auxerre. When he arrived it became even more difficult to fathom. He was absolutely brilliant. The question seemed to be not if, but when, he would move. This was to prove prescient.

I was invited to join the board of the Supporters' Trust in October 2004. I wasn't sure what responsibilities they envisioned for me, and for the first few months I didn't do much bar attend board meetings and hand out leaflets. This seemed a very do-able proposition for me. So long as I could help, I was happy to. On the field we started well but then hit a dodgy spell, which led to a make-or-break match with Maritimo of Portugal to gain entry to the newly formed UEFA Cup group stages. There was talk that failure to progress would lead to McLeish being dismissed. It was a tense night all right, but we eventually made it after a penalty shoot-out. From that, confidence seemed to spread throughout the team and we began to look capable of winning things. We knocked Celtic out of the League Cup at Ibrox after our first win against them in six matches. Things began to move forward from there.

The on-going growth of fans' culture was noticeable this season. People started using Follow Follow as the place to get their Rangers news. It was

149

as if they had realised that there was no place in the mainstream for Rangers fans, so we would simply create our own universe. It's punk rock – if you won't give us what we want, we will do it ourselves. People began to organise meets, and there was a definite unification of different aspects of the support. The Blue Order formed the first singing section at Ibrox to try to help create a better atmosphere within the stadium. This was, to me, totemic of what was going on with the support. No longer were fans just prepared to sit back and moan about what should be done. If something was annoying them and they felt they needed to take action, they did so. If no one would support them, they'd just do it themselves. The Blue Order brought some of the best aspects of European fan culture to Scotland, with an arch sense of humour and fantastic displays of colour. They organised and did the work for stadium-wide card displays, which looked astonishing. They deserve a hell of a lot of credit as far as I am concerned.

Moves were afoot behind the scenes, too. On 1 September 2004 Murray announced his return to the chairmanship, and with it a rights-issue to raise the funds with which to reduce – and ultimately eliminate – the club's debt. Murray underwrote the share issue to the tune of £50 million, an impressive sum of money no matter where it went (rumours speculated it had simply been moved to another area of Murray International Holdings). In doing so Murray also saw his shareholding in the club increase to around 92 per cent of the total stock. This meant it was his club, lock, stock and barrel. Why did he do this? The Trust had campaigned long and loudly that he should come back and sort out the mess he had created. It was speculated that Rangers' bankers felt he should come back and oversee matters on a day-to-day basis. The fans pumped in a lowly £2 million from the share issue, clearly because they agreed who should be assigned cleaning duties in any financial clear-up. This was Murray's mess. It was his job to try to bring some order back to Rangers' otherwise chaotic spending.

In January 2005 Boumsong was sold to Newcastle for £8 million. This had been coming. He'd complained about being abused by fans following a shockingly bad 2–0 defeat to Auxerre, which eliminated us from the UEFA Cup. Did it happen? Who knows. It did clear the decks for him to leave and circumvent UEFA's rule that states a player cannot move within 12 months of a Bosman transfer. Rangers did at least reinvest the money, bringing in Dutch goalkeeper Ronald Waterrus, Belgian midfielder Thomas Buffel and, shockingly, Barry Ferguson. Ferguson had been as miserable as sin down there and hankered after a return ticket home. Fans were split on the signing, given how he had agitated for a move 18 months before. I was happy, though I could see their point. Some never really forgave him. It led to a solidification of the arguments between supporters. Some would laud Ferguson no matter what he did, for others he could do no right. The truth, as always, was somewhere in the middle. He never scaled the heights he had in his first spell but did prove a valuable signing.

In March of that season we played Motherwell in the League Cup Final. It marked 10 years to the month since the great Davie Cooper had died, tragically young, of a brain haemorrhage. As Coop had starred for both clubs with great distinction, it was decided by the fans that this match would be a tribute to the sublime wingman. Spiers weighed in with his usual classy contribution, writing an article saying that Coop really wasn't that good and he didn't know what the fuss was about. It was the sort of thing that you'd expect from a particularly virulent Celtic fanzine. Actually, I take that back; Celtic fans wouldn't have tried to piss on the memory of a great man. They have a bit more dignity than that. Spiers' increasingly desperate attempts to shock were becoming as tedious and tiresome as a toddler demanding sweets. Sadly, his writing was on a par with an infant's too. Getting through one of his articles was like pushing a car up a hill with the handbrake on.

We won the match 5–1 in what was a glorious day at Hampden. However, it looked like this could be the only silverware we won that year. Celtic had brought Craig Bellamy in on loan from Newcastle and he looked every inch what he was; an English Premier League player running riot in a lesser League. We beat them 2–0 at Parkhead, our first win there in five years, but they beat us at Ibrox thanks to a virtuoso display from the Welshman. He was a cock of a human being, but you couldn't deny he could turn it on when he needed to. There's nothing worse than someone who talks smack but can back it up. When they won the match at the 'Brox it put them five points clear with four games to go. A couple of Celtic fans unfurled a banner saying, 'We won the League at Ibrox'.

It did look that way. I had given up, mentally. Still, the players got themselves up for the run-in, winning a tricky game against Aberdeen despite atrocious conditions. Being forced to play at Pittodrie would probably count as atrocious anyway, but it was a savage day in terms of weather. A Prso-inspired Rangers gritted their teeth and got on with it. Celtic, improbably, began to slip up. They dropped points in successive matches against Hibs and Hearts. Some Rangers fans began to dream of an unlikely comeback victory. I didn't. I had prepared my head for the defeat and the ongoing summer. I was not about to set myself up for more disappointment.

The events of 22 May 2005 are seared onto the psyche of any Old Firm fan. Rangers had to win against Hibs at Easter Road and hope Celtic didn't against Motherwell at Fir Park. I couldn't get a ticket for Easter Road. There was a groundswell of optimism on Follow Follow, but I didn't share it. Big Marv said he had spoken to God and was sure we were going to win. 'Keep believing,' he said. I wanted to, but I just couldn't. Scot and I went to a pub in the south side to watch it. As both games were being broadcast simultaneously, pubs had got together and agreed who would show each game to avoid crowds mixing and potential for bother. We were in The Corona in Shawlands, which was full of Bears. I wouldn't say the atmosphere was particularly hopeful, especially when Celtic scored midway through the first half.

We scored early in the second half through wee Nacho, but time ticked on without it looking like anything was going to change. Bellamy could have put it to bed earlier but had missed a series of one-on-ones with the Motherwell 'keeper. I suspected this was just to keep the lightest flame of belief going in the Rangers support before cruelly extinguishing it in the last minute. As John Cleese said, it's not the despair, it's the hope. Hibs only needed to avoid a heavy defeat to cement their place in Europe, so a sort of mini Germany versus Austria 1982 scenario unfolded. We passed the ball about in our half. They milled about in their half. Nothing happened. Time marched on. Scot asked me if I fancied going for something to eat. I couldn't face it. The town would be filled with celebrating Tims. I was for sitting in front of the telly that night, getting more sourly drunk.

An old guy was sitting on his own in the pub with headphones on, listening to the Celtic game. He turned round and said, quite casually, Motherwell have scored. I didn't think I'd heard him correctly. The next thing the Rangers End on the massive screen was going barmy. The TV pictures flashed up Motherwell scoring with just a few minutes left. The pub's collective heartbeat seemed suddenly audible, beating at a ferocious pace. The old guy was impassive.

When he turned round a minute later and coolly said, 'It's 2–1,' my heart sank. I assumed he'd meant to Celtic. But then the Rangers End on the screen erupted again. The pictures came up from Fir Park and Motherwell had, indeed, made it 2–1. The ref blew at Easter Road. Improbably, we had won the League, a League that was heading to Parkhead with only three minutes of the season to go. When the title race goes to the last day, the SPL hire a helicopter to deliver the trophy to whoever wins it, so that the presentation can take place that day. Radio Clyde's Peter Martin famously exclaimed, 'The helicopter is changing direction!' when the second goal went in at Fir Park. The day would forever be known as 'Helicopter Sunday'.

We immediately changed our plans and decided to have a few drinks in another pub that had a beer garden before heading over to Ibrox. You could spot who supported which team simply by sight. The Rangers fans had enormous, inane grins that couldn't be removed with a chisel. The Celtic fans staggered unbelievingly, their faces either contorted in horror or **153** frozen in a thousand-yard stare. Scot and I bounced into another pub, and as we did a Celtic fan started crying and had to be physically helped out of the bar by his girlfriend. The best moment came when a mini-bus let out across the road from us and disconsolate Celtic fans tripped out of it. One had a t-shirt that read 'Celtic: Premier League Champions 2004–2005'. I didn't know whether to laugh or laugh really hard.

We went to Ibrox that night to see the team and trophy with around 30,000 others. It was a landmark, never-to-be-forgotten day for the support. However, dark clouds were having into the horizon and would soon threaten the whole club.

13

Media Man

That summer saw Martin O'Neill leave Celtic, to be replaced by Gordon Strachan. I'd quite liked Strachan as a pundit so I was a wee bit disappointed to see him join the cloven-hoofed ones. The Celtic fans went into open mourning at losing O'Neill. He was everything they'd wanted in a Celtic manager. He was Irish, Catholic and mildly successful. We added a few new players, such as Nieto, Fan-Fan, Rodriguez and Murray, and looked to have a decent side in place to retain the title. It looked good.

There was also some reorganisation at the Trust. Colin Glass left due to family reasons, and in the ensuing shuffle my friend Stephen Smith and I were assigned the media role. Stephen is a trade union official with a Che Guevara tattoo and passionately believes in his principles. He is about as far removed from the stereotypical view of a Rangers fan as you can get. His hobbies include the music of Bruce Springsteen, Krav Maga (a form of hand-to-hand combat) and falconry. He is the one-man Bolshevik contingent of his village near Birmingham, fighting a solo campaign to get the local shop to carry *The Guardian*. He's scarily bright – I rarely argue with him, because I never win. With Mark Dingwall on one side and him on the other, I often found myself as the football in a political struggle. I love both of them dearly. Of course, it doesn't make sense to some that him and Dingwall, a modern-day Lenin and Mussolini, can be such great friends, but that's the way it is in the Rangers support. We're not a monoculture.

The Trust's media hadn't been the best to this point. Our press releases were somewhat long and rambling, which lessened their chances of publication. We also sent out far too many. In my five years in the media team, we've only sent out half a dozen releases. The rest of our comment has been invited. Stephen understood how it worked, having created press releases in his job for a number of years. I could see what he brought to the table, but I couldn't quite see how I was going to help. Stephen's rationale was simple; he felt we needed a mouthy wee sod who wasn't afraid to shout about his allegiances. I was qualified for this role, eminently so.

The season started well, with a superb 3–1 win against Celtic and qualification for the Champions League. We comfortably got through against old foes Anorthosis Famagusta, Prso and Buffel being the key men. Celtic had suffered a humiliating Champions League exit at the hands of Artmedia Bratislava. They had been royally rogered 5–0 over there, and had, in fact, appeared to give up at 3–0. This was to prove costly, as they won the return match 4–0. Scot and I followed the first match in a restaurant with our wives. Every time somebody went to the to the toilet, it seemed they'd conceded another goal. The Old Firm game saw Alan Thompson sent off after half an hour, Rangers dominate Celtic and Neil Lennon try to attack the ref after the match had ended. This Old Firm game also saw the first time I appeared on radio.

Ewen Cameron had been approached about his Real Radio football phone-in featuring supporters as guests. He, uniquely in the Scottish media, saw this as a good idea. Most media pundits hate the idea of fans getting in on their racket. Their idea is that fans listen, presenters talk. It has always been this way and should, therefore, always be this way. The idea of a mere layman coming in and talking about the game is anathema to them. Never mind that some ex-players are barely sentient, never mind that some seem to struggle with English as a first language. They played the game, they know more about it. Our job is to shut up, listen and pay into games.

Cameron came from a fans' perspective, however, and is something of the black sheep of the Scottish media because he does things his own way. He doesn't run in any cliques and does what he thinks is right. I like Ewen for that; he has integrity. No matter what you think of his show, it comes without any half-baked agenda. Therefore, when he called and asked if I would take part in an Old Firm special before the game, I accepted. The Celtic representative would be Tommy Dornan, a nice man. I had worn a suit. Yes, to do the radio. Tommy had done this before and came dressed for comfort in joggies. Suit on for match-day; it's the Rangers way. 1–0 before a ball was kicked. I had to get off to a good start.

I was incredibly nervous sitting in the cab over there. This was not helped by having a mental taxi driver, who was going through a messy divorce and insisted on sharing his woes with me. And there were a lot of them. No wonder his wife left him. Twenty minutes in his cab and I was contemplating self-harming. Or harming him.

What I really did want was to stand up and say 'I am a Rangers fan and I'm proud to be one.' I wanted to be articulate and represent us well. Of course, nerves would play a big part in it, but I think I did OK. I settled in and got comfortable through some middling calls. Then an idiot claiming to be a Rangers fan called in. He said that, although he was a Rangers fan, we were all bigots and the club should basically be shut down because of it. I bitch-slapped him verbally, which wasn't difficult because as the man was a pillock. Soon a few Celtic fans came on to have a go. Again, not much of a contest. The wild jungles of Follow Follow had schooled me well. I knew how to argue viciously. I didn't go after Tommy, because he was fundamentally a sound guy who'd just been born with an affliction, namely a love for Celtic. We can't all be lucky. The only jibe I got in was about Seville, when he mentioned the mystical 80,000 figure. I suggested he was using the Seville Calculator. He was rather indignant and said that it had been the largest mass migration in post-war European history. I pointed out that it was a shame it hadn't been the largest post-war mass emigration. I got in trouble with Victoria, the producer for that. That was the first, but not the last time that would happen.

The reaction from Rangers fans was incredibly heartening and not a little flattering. It was only later that I realised why. It wasn't specifically me they were responding to, rather the fact that someone was finally saying the things that they had wanted to. Rangers fans had been excluded from the debate for years. We weren't being called to give evidence at our own trial. It was simply, 'You are bigots, now bugger off and give us peace while we think of ways to punish you.' This allowed us to show a different side of the support. I think it was an important step in the direction of parity. A graph of how Rangers fans were being treated in the years 2000–10 would resemble a U-shape. Ewen Cameron deserves praise for his part in granting fans a voice, and he actually did more to erase bigotry than any of the so-called crusaders. This was because the one-sided moralisers had no credence with the support. The fact that they pilloried Rangers for merely existing meant fans disregarded everything they said. Their presence only hardened attitudes. By allowing a voice for more moderate media coverage to take hold, Ewen helped usher in a climate where argument could take place. You are far more likely to change opinions through education and debate than abuse and dictates. Fans will listen to others' opinions when they think the same courtesy is being extended back to them. It's not perfect yet, but it is better. Rangers fans are not universally liked, but we accept that. All we want is the same level playing field as everyone else gets. It's simply justice.

My friends in the Neptune Bar on match days were not going to allow me to get too big for my boots. Scot offered an honest critique. Tommy and Ian B said I had done well, but was still a fanny. Odin disagreed, saying I was a fanny who still never bought anyone a drink. This was, I am sure, said with love. Of sorts. It had been an enjoyable experience, one that I thought would be a one-off. To clear up one thing about any media work, no, you don't get paid for it. You don't paid for being in the papers, on the radio or on the TV. It's voluntary. So anyone who suspects that fans reps turn up on these things for cash is wrong. Occasionally the BBC will offer you a nominal payment if you are on a show for a considerable length of time. I think it is in their charter that they have to. But that is extremely rare. I think in five years of doing this, I was paid four times. They were not life-changing sums of money.

The last few months of 2005 were the most bizarre that many of us had experienced. We'd suddenly fallen apart domestically and began to undergo the longest run we'd ever been on without a win. And it just stretched on and on. We were useless, and it didn't matter who we played. Scot and I travelled through to watch us play unfashionable Livingston, a nice place to watch your football. You could park easily, there were plenty of places to eat and you could wear colours without a Neanderthal bouncer barring you from spending your money. Alas, we couldn't actually score. Or create a chance. It was two hours of distinct nothingness. This wouldn't be our only away trip where that happened. This game was marked out by the strange case of Almondvale's missing toilets. Rangers took up three of the ends of the stadium – and some said Livvy were a made-up club with no fanbase – but the toilets seemed to have been designed by a watersports fetishist for his own amusement. I joined a massive queue and, as I got nearer the front, did what men do in these circumstances; I began preparations towards getting my lad out and being ready to commence the jet as soon as I was in sight of the urinal. Sadly, when I got up there, tackle out, I noticed, too late, that there was no urinal. It was a wall. Displaying the mentality of the Scottish football fan, namely 'they are going over there so that must be the way', had led me to this. Obviously frustrated, a gang of guys had just started pissing against a wall. Others followed, soon there was a queue, and now this. It was too late by then, though. I was now locked into the initiation sequence with no override button. I peed. Apologies to the Livvy cleaning staff. Judging by the small lake of recently drank lager that was pooling on the floor, my contribution didn't affect the situation too much.

In the midst of this run, we began to build up a head of steam in the Champions League. The matches were superbly exciting, if lacking a little in quality. We beat Porto 3–2 in a thrilling game most memorable for Prso slamming the 'keeper into the net for a goal and getting away with it. We then lost 1–0 to Inter Milan in the San Siro, a match played behind closed doors due to the Inter fans injuring Anders Frisk with a coin after a poor display in the previous seasons Champions League. That game was memorable for the eerie silence in the stadium, which was only enlivened by some Rangers fans singing *The Sash*. Yes, some got in. Simon from the Trust and Blue Order wore a suit to the game and pretended to be an official of the club, and they let him in. We then drew twice with Celtic's conquerors, Artmedia, before a goal from youngster Ross McCormack gained us an undeserved draw in Porto. McCormack was punted by us at the end of the season on the very reasonable grounds that he was gash. I couldn't stand the rat-like winger and had no idea why. I kept my counsel on it – it's offside to slag a young player simply on a hunch. He then did well at Cardiff and got in the Scotland side, where he treated us to a rhapsody about how he'd always been a Celtic fan and would love to play for them. I knew it. They are welcome to the penalty-taking pie muncher.

Despite having just the one win, our three draws had made it possible for us to qualify if our last result (against Inter) matched Artmedia's (against Porto). Inter had already made it through and, frankly, couldn't give a toss about the last match. God bless Italian teams and their professional mentality. This Rangers side contained Bob Malcolm, Hamed Namouchi and Franny Jeffers. It is fair to say that better teams from Scotland had tried to escape the Champions League group stages, but all had failed. This one didn't. Inside a frenetic Ibrox – frenetic at our end, at least, few Italians having bothered to travel for what was, for them, a dead rubber – we got our draw, a first for Scotland and for Rangers. Some of our fans took blow-up European Cups to the next Old Firm game to taunt Celtic supporters. This, of course, made the Celtic fans howl with laughter, as they had won the bloody thing and we hadn't.

Despite this remarkable achievement, however, we continued to get worse. I started to get asked for comment by various newspapers, which I did as soberly as I could. I didn't want to slag the team off in public, nor was it appropriate. My problem with Rangers' performance was in the off-the-field area. Rangers had never, not once, defended their fans against the ludicrous charges that the media had thrown our way. Not once. They had never listened to the fans' warnings about where the financial mismanagement was taking us. The chairman was presiding over a poor run, where Celtic had overtaken us from a standing start. Even this season, defending our title with Celtic having a new manager in charge, we had failed to maintain the advantage. The League was almost over already.

Murray had to act. He simply had no option. As the criticism grew ever stronger he announced in November that he would look at McLeish's performance in the next five matches; if things didn't improve, he would look at the situation again and an announcement would be made on 5 December. This, at last, was leadership. You see, for all the criticism Murray received in the noughties, Rangers fans still wanted to like him. We wanted him to be the dynamic leader of the 1990s, only without the silly spending habits. The clapped-out, tired and clearly sick-of-it chairman of the new decade was not the guy we'd grown up with. You could say it was harsh on Eck, and it probably was; however, it happens in every other area of life on a daily basis. If your performance doesn't match expectations, then there's a chance you'll be out of work soon. It's not pleasant, and it's happened to me, but it's life. It was very clear what he needed to do – get results.

In those five games we drew three and lost two. The last of these draws was probably the worst of the lot. We were 2–0 up against Falkirk, who hadn't won since Oasis were good, and drew 2–2. The fans that day entered a new state of agitation. It was rage, horror and disgust merged into one combustible force. There was a protest outside. Rangers fans don't protest, as a rule. They usually feel it isn't the 'Rangers way'. There are times when we really should have been more ready to play this card. It shows the depth of feeling that the result that day caused a spontaneous eruption. It was all over for Eck. David Murray gathered his media poodles together on the Tuesday, and in an exclusive interview with Chic Young – Mr Murray, you have to judge men by the company they keep – he made the announcement: Eck was staying.

Pardon? How did that happen?

Murray had apparently discussed the situation with Eck and had asked him outright if he felt he was still the man for the job. Eck, somewhat understandably, said that yes, in fact, he was. The chairman said he then 'looked into his eyes' and knew that he was the man to take us forward. I didn't get it and, speaking to other Bears, I wasn't alone. He'd been failing all season, given five games to stop failing, continued to fail and now his reward was being kept on? I was beyond angry. I was bloody livid. At this point Ewen Cameron asked me if I'd like to come on the show that night. Probably not in the best mind to participate, I agreed. I gave Murray it tight. I really went to town on him, calling his leadership a shambles, pointing out his continued failure over the last half-decade, his broken promises, the financial mess, the lot. It was not the done thing. David Murray simply did not get criticised in the Scottish media. A lot of fans called to have a go at me, calling me 'ungrateful'. That gets right on my nipple ends, when football fans walk around on their knees like that. I pay into the matches. I contribute. So does every other fan who pays in to their football club. We can appreciate the efforts of the owners, but never should we be prone in front of them, arms outstretched for being so kind to us. I wonder why these people feel we have to be so supine. A lot of fans called to agree with me. It got heated between the two camps. Some simply felt we shouldn't be airing our dirty washing in public. I understood that but felt that this attitude was what had allowed Murray such a free run as he took us into chaos.

Murray called the next day and invited (demanded) me to attend a meeting with him in Charlotte Square. Mark came with me, although looking back it was not the wisest choice on one level. Murray and Mark didn't get on that well. However, Mark was not going to be intimidated by anyone. I knew there was a fair-to-middling chance I would be. Let's be honest here, I'm just a wee punter and the chairman was asking to see me. He is also an incredibly imposing man. He's built like a tank and just oozes charisma. You can see, pretty much instantly, why he is a captain of industry and you are not.

But — and this was a big but — I knew I was right. I had to stick to my guns. The structure of the meeting was one I would soon come to recognise:

Introductions:	Chairman makes a sarcastic remark about my media work. I just smile.
First 20 minutes:	Chairman swears at me a fair bit, and calls me names. I call him a few back.
Middle 20 minutes:	Chairman relaxes stance, says we are all in this together. Me, desperate to get out of the name-calling stage, grab at the lifeline. We are soon all Rangers fans together.
Last 20 minutes:	We allow Chairman to spin us a spiel in which we are on the verge of the European Cup. He does this in an extremely convincing fashion. We then leave, feeling great. An hour later we realise he hasn't actually told us how this transformation will occur.

That's pretty much the gist of it. As we walked in he was on a telephone barking commands but motioned for us to sit down. It all sounded outlandishly high-profile to me, sort of Gordon Gecko buy/sell language. When he had finished, he said 'that's me just concluded a £25 million deal. That's the kind of thing I do in a day.' Somehow remaining uncowed in the face of this place-putting, Mark mischievously replied, 'Great! Who we signing?' When the chairman replied that it was a property deal, Mark pointed out that he really didn't know much about the chairman's other interests and cared even less. We were here to talk about Rangers. That's the problem with alpha males. They assume everyone else is motivated by what they are motivated by. I don't care what car someone drives. I've never bothered learning to drive so Fiesta or a Ferrari makes no odds to me! My idea of hell is to work 70-hour weeks closing deals and touching base. I worked for 10 years in the recruitment industry, which I loathed. I was good at it because there isn't really much to it. But I met enough of proto-*Apprentice* contestants to realise that there was more to life. Christ, there has to be.

Murray did freak me out a bit when he listed where I worked, where I lived, who I was married to, who my parents were and what school I'd gone to. I'd like to say I was nonchalant, but this was a new world to me. I just wanted us to be a bit better at set-pieces, for crying out loud.

The media work was going through the roof. Requests were taken on an individual basis before we decided if we would use it. The media in Scotland is simple enough; some are Tims and don't care who knows it, some are Bears and do care who knows it, and some just can't be arsed with all the crap and see it as a job. The *Herald* and Radio Clyde, due to being for Celts by Celts, were both ignored. We got to know the good guys in the Scottish media, the ones you could trust – Neil Cameron and Colin Duncan at the *Record*, Derek McGregor and Gerry Duffy at *The Sun*, Daryl King at the *Evening Times*, Jim Spence at the BBC and Ronnie Esplin at the Press Association being among the best.

I started to get some unwelcome attention at this time. It became fairly routine to get some idiots on the mobile who were planning, by their own accounts, on doing me in. One favourite was the chap who said he knew where my kids went to school. I don't have any kids. To be honest, it got a little childish. I would deliberately wind up the Tims, and the more nutty ones in their support would phone and offer to kill me. One wee guy did this brilliantly. He called and I answered by saying 'David Edgar?' He replied, 'Is that David Edgar?' (That's the time-honoured 'moron-on-a-phone-in' response – 'Can I speak to the panel please?' 'No, in a change to the advertised format, instead we're going to make you talk to Mark Lawson about the shortlist for the Booker prize.' Who the hell else do you think you'll be speaking to?) He then told me he was going to kill me. I pointed out he hadn't dialled from an anonymous number and thus I had his mobile number. Was this a wind-up threat or one I had to report to the police? It wasn't, he assured me. I asked his name. He said he was called Paul. I asked Paul if his Mum would be proud of him calling up strangers and offering to kill them. No, he admitted, she wouldn't. I told him I was going to hang up but I didn't want him calling me back. He thanked me, and told me I was doing a good job for the Trust. I almost wet myself.

Eck was being given the chance to lead us into the last-16 clash with Villarreal. There was a certain natural justice to that as he had led us into the competition. The football practicalities kicked in though. What we were doing was basically giving up the season to let Eck have his day in the sun. We started to play a bit better, aided by the arrival of Kris Boyd from Kilmarnock in Jan 2006. We then dropped back to mediocre levels. By the time of the Villarreal match, we basically had this left to play for, and that was it. Celtic had played Villarreal a few years before and were twinned with them. They had a made a big paella on the beach with them or something. We had the papers running stories on how Celtic fans were backing Villrreal because of their special relationship. We could have been playing The Adolf Hitler Memorial XI and they would have got support from our rivals.

The first leg at Ibrox ended 2–2. We played really well, but you could see that this was a quality team we were up against. It was the first night I have heard a crowd make a substitution, with Eck having to bow to the braying demands that he put Buffel on. Ibrox was rewarded when the Belgian supplied the ball that led to the equaliser. The away leg was to prove an eventful trip. I couldn't get time off, so it was TV for me. I received a call from Real Radio during the day asking me if I could put them in touch with a fan over there for a chat. They got an extremely inebriated Odin. He did well, though – given his ludicrous Fife accent, he sounds drunk most of the time anyway. Just joking, Fifers!

Rangers fans just took over the whole area. Despite a meagre ticket allowance, the away support outnumbered the home support three to one. Villarreal is not a footballing hotbed, and many locals saw it as a chance to make some easy cash on a match that was live on the TV, with tickets going for up to 10-times face value. The Villarreal team bus had a window smashed by a bottle thrown by a Rangers fan. This is thuggish and unacceptable. A lot of incidents involving British teams, and especially Rangers, are alcohol-fuelled. There is a suicide drinking culture of fans hitting the booze hard from the moment they get up until the moment they pass out. This is not unique to Rangers fans but is embraced by us. In this case, trip to Spain plus cheap booze and sun equalled moronic behaviour.

The match finished 1–1, with Rangers playing shockingly well, easily our best performance of the season. We were incredibly unlucky not to progress, with Boyd missing a straightforward chance to put us through near the end. To lose on away goals to a quality side like Villarreal was no humiliation. The fun was just starting though.

UEFA announced that they had received complaints about chants emanating from the away fans in the second leg. When pressed, they admitted that these complaints had come from Scotland. There had been an orchestrated campaign on some Celtic websites to get people to watch the game and then contact UEFA to swoon in horror and demand action. What sort of human being goes out of their way to be offended? On its own, however, UEFA would have simply ignored these malcontent social misfits. The deciding factor in taking action was the interference from some Scottish MSPs, Irish politicians and Scottish journalists. Yes, they had concocted a little plan to get Rangers into trouble. This is what MSPs felt was a valuable use of their time. This is what MSPs felt was beneficial to society. This was what they had been elected to do. No wonder we're

screwed.

UEFA took evidence from the club and from their own prosecutor, a man called Gerhard Kapl, who was getting his information straight from a certain broadsheet journalist and his loony pals in the kiddy Parliament. In the end, they decided – rightly – that they really didn't want to get involved in this idiotic mudslinging in a parochial backwater and fined us for the broken window, noting that sectarianism was a local problem and, frankly, we were welcome to it. I was in the BBC green room waiting to go on air with Graham Spiers when the decision broke. The memory of his face as he was told – he even asked the reporter to check – still gives me a semi. I had the time of my life on the radio show. I was actually quite magnanimous. He looked a broken man, although I've no idea why, him being a neutral journalist and all.

However, I'd celebrated too early. UEFA appealed their own decision and Kapl, a devout Catholic being fed tales of us burning chapels, pretty much threatened to cause ruptions if we weren't punished. To keep him happy, they hit us with a fine and banned the singing of *The Billy Boys*. There was an outcry from the fans. This was our anthem. The contentious line in it was 'we are up to our knees in Fenian blood'. Debate raged on what that meant. Some commentators said we used it to mean 'Catholic'. Rangers fans argued that it was instead a reference to a gang who were enemies of the British state, the original Fenians. If you go on Celtic fan boards, you'll see merchandise for sale that says 'unrepentant Fenian bastard'. My take on it? Some people probably did use it to mean Catholic. Some probably did use it to mean enemies of their country. And most sang it just because it was a song that had been sung for decades, which was rousing in a football stadium.

I'd agree that it's not very nice to be singing about wading through anyone's blood. Kilmarnock fans sing a version in which they are 'up to their knees in Ayr blood'. Nobody has a problem with that. It seems it is religiously motivated blood which causes the issue. The club accepted the ban, and began to wonder how they'd get it done. Now they wanted to be our pals. We were summoned for several meetings at which we gave suggestions on what to do. I signed off on a document by the club and fans' groups encouraging supporters not to sing it. This was not popular. I still get people coming up to me accusing me of selling out. As far as I was concerned, the battle died the second the club accepted the decision. Fans wanted us to take this to court, not quite realising that if the club had accepted it, then that was it. My view was that if the club was going to be punished for the singing of the song – which it was – then we had to stop singing it. That was the realpolitik of the situation.

Of course, the original idea behind this whole thing wasn't to help battle sectarianism. Those who had been involved wanted Rangers punished, end of. They collectively wet themselves at the thought of Rangers fans singing this song and being in more hot water. And you know what? The Rangers fans won. They stopped singing it, almost overnight. The disappointment from those in the media who were behind it was palpable.

So, onwards and upwards. Our pitiful domestic campaign finally died on its arse with a 3–0 tonking from Hibs at Ibrox in the Cup. The fans were apoplectic. We'd not just been beaten, we'd been annihilated. McLeish had played a mad 4–2–4 formation and Hibs had dominated us in midfield. There was a huge demo outside. Scot and Mark were pictured at it, which persuaded Murray that the Trust were behind it. We weren't. My presence across the media in the next couple of days enraged him further. The Trust chairman, Malcolm McNiven, was called in to see Murray and was lambasted about allowing me to spout such crazy things as my opinion. At that moment, I appeared on *Reporting Scotland* and came on the TV in Murray's office. Malcolm told me he screamed, 'That bastard is everywhere!' as my face filled the screen. A meeting was set for Thursday morning, at which I'd be verbally beaten up by the chairman.

Circumstances overtook this, however. We played Aberdeen on Wednesday at Pittodrie. They humped us 2–0, with Eck persisting with his crazy 4–2–4 formation. I always knew how much trouble I am in at Ibrox depending on where the meeting is. Blue room – fine; chairman's office – some shouting; manager's office – bollocking. This had been downgraded to the chairman's office. Murray was almost penitent. He still had a go at me for criticising the club. I pointed out that I hadn't, I'd been criticising him. That was something we fundamentally disagreed on. He felt that any criticism of him was a criticism of the club. I didn't. Murray also felt that the best way to deal with criticism is to deal with the person who made it, not the content. If Rangers put half as much energy into dealing with complaints as it does into rubbishing the complainer, we'd all be better off. We discussed the situation for a while. Eventually, he took a car to Murray Park and announced that McLeish would be replaced at the end of the season.

Eck had done very well in his time at Rangers, but that era was over. He'd go on, with Scotland and Birmingham, to prove what a good manager he was, but it was time to move on. The person who we turned to was, unbelievably, Paul Le Guen. He was the hottest young manager in Europe at the time, after several years success with perennial French champs, Lyon. I am not sure how Murray persuaded him, but persuade him he did. Our own Arsene Wenger! After the help with *The Billy Boys*, the club and the Trust had a good relationship, and they actually let us break the news of his arrival at our annual dinner. Excitement was high indeed. We won the proverbial sweet FA that season, but we were poised to go into the new season on a high. What a season it would prove to be – but not for the reasons we thought.

14

Red, White and Blue Tsunami

The summer didn't bring in the expected overhaul of players. Le Guen spent very little, around £3 million, on a collection of somewhat unheralded players. Karl Svensson, a timid centre-half, arrived from IFK Gothenburg. Czech winger Libor Sionko became the first of a trio of players who arrived from Vienna, followed quickly by striker Filip Sebo and defender Sasa Papac. Goalkeeper Lionel Letizi arrived to replace the departing Stefan Klos. There were also a few youngsters and loan signings. It looked like a mixed bunch, but we believed he knew what he was doing. His track record suggested he did, after all.

I met him at a meeting at Murray Park. He seemed confident and assured. He spoke about his desire to bring in a fluent, continental-style passing game. He spoke about the players' diets. It all seemed positive, modern football management. And it started very well, with an excellent display against Motherwell at Fir Park bringing a 2–1 victory. We played really, really well that day. You could see what he was trying to achieve, and the atmosphere among fans in the away ends that day was pretty much unbridled optimism. After that, however, it started to deteriorate rapidly. We drew 2–2 with Dundee United the following week. It became clear that we could not deal with set-pieces. Anything into our box was a potential goal. He panicked, putting Brahim Hemdani in there. Hemdani was a good footballer but nervy at centre-back. The results began to grow poorer and poorer. Celtic had signed Kenny Miller – Judas – and he broke his duck for them against us in a terrible 2–0 defeat at Parkhead. Le Guen seemed unable to stop the rot. There was talk of massive dressing room unrest. Reports suggested that the players and the manager didn't get on and that he felt undermined by a group of Scottish players, whose complaints included him banning Monster Munch and other such snacks at the training ground. Poor results against Falkirk, St Mirren and Hibs followed. We drew at Kilmarnock thanks to a last-minute penalty conceded by Alan Hutton and scored by Stevie Naismith. Rumours swirled that he had offered his resignation in October after we were knocked out of the League Cup at home by First Division St Johnstone, the first time we'd ever lost at home to a lower division side.

I was offered a column by the *Daily Record* at this point. It fell through because they couldn't get a Celtic fan to write a balancing one. The *Record* were pretty scared of offending the Celtic support at this point. The *Record* had printed a story about Celtic players going on the rampage at a Christmas night out, which they had headlined 'Thugs and Thieves'. This had infuriated both players and supporters. The way Celtic played this was beautiful. They didn't respond, save by flashing up an image of the front page at every home game. Celtic fans got the message – real fans don't buy the *Record*. I admired Celtic greatly for this stance. Rangers could have learned a lot from them at this point. Of course, this ability would soon lead to hubris at Celtic and play a big part in their fall from eminence. My only regret is that the *Record* got me in for some photographs to publicise it. They still use those photographs when I feature in the paper. I was three stone heavier then, and people still think I'm a tubby because of those photographs.

At this time I started working for a company who rented an office from Paul McStay. Yes, that Paul McStay, formerly of Celtic. He now ran a graphic design company and was therefore in the office all day. You'd meet him in the kitchen when making coffee. If it was cool for me to be able to talk to him about football, imagine what it was like for Liam. After a while it became commonplace, so much so that you'd be talking about the game the previous night and Paul would say something. You'd go to disagree, then you'd remember he had 70 caps and a hatful of medals, and therefore knew more about football than you did. When the World Cup 2006 began, Liam and I bugged Paul into getting a freeview box for the TV in the boardroom. He did so, and we used to have the privilege of watching football matches with our own expert summariser. Listening to him was an education as he told us what managers were doing, why it worked or didn't and what teams would need to do to change things. Paul is one of the nicest people in the world, it is as simple as that. He bought me a wedding present – I was very proud of that! Why Celtic are employing another ex-midfielder with a quarter of his talent is beyond me. For me, he's been a huge loss to the Scottish game.

December saw us reach a nadir. After a creditable 1–1 draw with Celtic at Ibrox, which left us 15 points behind our rivals by January, we lost 2–1 to Inverness. We followed this up with a tame 1–1 draw at home to St Mirren. Over the Christmas and New Year period all hell broke loose. Le Guen stripped Barry Ferguson of the captaincy and told him he would never play for the club again. Against Motherwell, Kris Boyd scored the only goal from the penalty spot and pointedly held up six fingers (Ferguson wore the number-six jersey). Civil war had engulfed Rangers. I was on holiday in Dunoon for the New Year fielding call after call. Murray stepped in and made the decision: the Frenchman would leave. Le Guen, to his immense credit, asked for no pay-off. Ferguson was immediately hailed by some fans as Mr Rangers, by others a poisonous influence who'd gotten too big for his boots. The fans were divided over this.

In the final analysis, Le Guen's results had been awful. He looked like a man who didn't want to be there, and to me, his decision over Ferguson was designed to engineer the situation that allowed him to leave. He was the right man at the wrong time. He'd been given little in the way of transfer funds, he was unable to stamp his authority on a group of unruly players and, fundamentally, he'd underestimated how tough it is to win in Scotland. It was a shame, a real shame, because he had the pedigree and the coaching chops to have been a real success for us. What pleased me was that nobody puts Le Guen's failure down to his religion. It simply wasn't an issue. Rangers' first Catholic manager had come and gone, the world remained resolutely on its axis and people seemed prepared to actually let us move on.

Who to turn to now? Credit to Murray, he moved very quickly. Walter Smith would be returning for a second spell, accompanied by Ally McCoist, who gave up a lucrative TV career to return. Interestingly, they were joined by Kenny McDowell, a former youth coach at Celtic. Walter had been the manager of Scotland and restored much needed stability after the embarrassing reign of Berti Vogts. He was criticised for leaving Scotland to rejoin Rangers, but it was understandable. This was his club and they didn't just want him, they actually needed him. How could he turn this down? Before Walter officially took charge, Dunfermline knocked us out of the Scottish Cup to ensure the next few months would be a series of dead rubbers. Walter brought in some actual defenders in Davie Weir, Ugo Ehiogu and Andy Webster, and Kevin Thomson to add some steel to midfield. We improved dramatically and achieved two enjoyable, albeit meaningless, wins over Celtic in the League.

Season 2007–08 would never be forgotten. Walter restructured the team, bringing in Lee McCulloch, Steven Naismith, Jean-Claude Darcheville, Carlos Cuéllar, Kirk Broadfoot and Daniel Cousin, among others. The team had a different look about them, one that was typical Walter – pragmatic. We had been a soft touch for too long. Now anyone who wanted to beat us would have to earn the privilege. We weren't scintillating, but we were effective. We had two nervy wins to get into the Champions League, over FC Zeta and Red Star Belgrade. Then we were there, in what appeared to be a group of death – for us – Lyon, Stuttgart and Barcelona.

We started well with a 2–1 comeback win over Stuttgart. Alan Hutton had been playing really well since Walter returned, but he was out of this world in the opening months of this season. That night he was fantastic, tearing the Germans apart on the overlap. Charlie Adam scored a beauty before Darcheville nabbed the winner from the penalty spot. Darcheville was instantly loved by the fans. He had an easy-going manner and a committed style. He was also the recipient of one of Archie MacPherson's mispronunciations. Archie is a Scottish institution, but he has grown ever more idiosyncratic as he gets older. He had a spell commentating for Eurosport about 20 years ago and has decided that this makes him an expert on pronunciation of foreign names. This generally involves him deciding on a crazy way of saying the name then sticking to it. In this case, Darcheville's name is pronounced 'darsh-vil'. Quite straightforward, really – far too straightforward for Archie. He decided instead he'd call him 'Darky-vee'. Thankfully someone seemed to notify him of the deeply inappropriate nature of that attempt and he compromised to the more politically palatable 'darshy-veel'.

Darcheville was also the recipient of an 'hilarious' chant from the Aberdeen fans that caught on with similarly brain-damaged away supports through the season – 'You're just a fat Eddie Murphy'. I'm not quite sure what the rationale behind this was. He didn't look like Eddie Murphy, talk like Eddie Murphy or in any way resemble Eddie Murphy apart from the fact that he was black. Were the Aberdeen fans not saying, basically, that all black men looked the same? I always wondered why no journalist, at the height of the 'let's get the Rangers fans' campaign, called me up about the 'Nakamura ate my dog' chant some Rangers fans used. I dreaded that call. Following the stereotype, this song would be aimed at a Korean player, which is bad enough, but singing it at a Japanese player is worse. It's basically perpetuating the idea that all people of Oriental extraction look the same. It rather reinforced my belief that the most strident media punters weren't interested in actually stopping offensive chanting. Here was a genuinely offensive chant and it was being ignored because they weren't looking for that. They wanted anti-Catholic and anti-Catholic only.

If that was a good result, the next one was stunning. We hammered Lyon, who hadn't lost at home in the Champions League. Not only that, but it was 3–0 going on five. It was an astonishing, shocking result. My friend Robbie has lived in France for years and said his French mates were in shock after it. So was I. Rob, myself and Cammy ended up out until 3am celebrating. On a Tuesday. I made an executive decision to go into work late the next day. Sky called and asked if I could do an interview live at 11am. I had a shower and a shave and headed to their studio. I was still pretty out of it as I did the interview. I was asked about Celtic's match with Milan that night and answered honestly: I hoped football would be the winner and, failing that, Milan. You can still see this on YouTube. I think it is a textbook example of being drunk but hiding it well.

We then had a double header against Barcelona. The club had set up 'fanzones' in the city on matchdays. I met my friend Ian and his son Stuart there before the home match. We chatted with some Barca fans, who asked how many Rangers fans would make the away trip in a fortnight. '20,000', we said. They couldn't believe it would be that many. We headed off to the match. Nothing really happened. They had Ronaldinho, Messi and Henry. We didn't. Bearing that in mind, we did what we had to and defended, and we got a 0–0 draw, a superb result. Afterwards a few Barca players accused us of 'anti-football'. I'm sorry we didn't just stand back and let you win. Dry your eyes. Football is about attacking and defending. Both parts have their place. We had seven points from nine. We were going through.

Disappointingly for the Scottish media, we didn't destroy Barcelona and ransack the Sagrada Família. The press were wondering how we'd be received in Barcelona, given what happened in at the Cup-Winners' Cup in 1972, completely missing the point. The Rangers fans had battered

Franco's riot police that night. The Catalonians loved us for it. On the pitch, we lost 2–0. We weren't humiliated, and it took Thierry Henry punching the ball in to give Barca the lead. Funnily enough, there was no call from Radio Clyde to have Henry banned from the game after that. Two years later he'd do it for France against the Republic of Ireland in a game meaning nothing in Scotland, and Clyde would devote three shows to it. And people have the audacity to suggest that Radio Clyde have an agenda!

I can't let this last point go without mentioning Hugh Keevins. Around this time he wrote that Ibrox resembled the Nuremberg Rallies because of the number of Union Jacks flown before big matches. Invoking something as horrific as a Nazi rally to slag off a football club really showed the bitterness and idiocy of some members of the press. Keevins was forced to apologise. How we laughed.

We lost 3–2 in Stuttgart, giving away some silly goals and leaving ourselves with a bit too much to do. This meant we needed a point against Lyon in our last match, which would be at home. We were losing 1–0 with five minutes left when Darcheville had an open goal. The whole stadium rose and then sat down in despair as he knocked it over the bar. Lyon scored two more on the counter to avenge their home tonking. We were out and into the UEFA Cup. It seemed scant consolation, though it proved not to be. In the League we were progressing well. We reached the League Cup Final, beating Hearts in the semi at Hampden on one of the coldest nights I can remember. We were going for the treble.

We met Panathinaikos in the UEFA Cup and drew 0–0 at home. It seemed a distraction from the League. The manager certainly gave that impression. However, a late Nacho Novo goal gave us an away-goals win. We then drew Werder Bremen, which was a very good side. After a dramatic 2–0 win at Ibrox, we held them down to a single-goal victory in Bremen thanks to a superb goalkeeping performance from Allan McGregor. At work the next day, the Celtic fans were giving me pelters for our team's lucky win. I told them that I was so confident of going all the way that I was booking a hotel room in Manchester for the night of the Final. I also applied for best tickets on the UEFA website. I would almost certainly still have been drunk when I did this and promptly forgot all about this until a week later, when the confirmation email came in from UEFA. £200 down the drain. There was no way we would reach the Final. That sort of thing just didn't happen to us. I began to wonder how I could list them on the German eBay if Bayern Munich made it. For some reason, though, I didn't cancel the tickets or hotel room. Maybe, just maybe we'd make it.

We had Sporting Lisbon in the quarters and again got a 0–0 draw in a dull match at Ibrox. We then went to play them in Lisbon. Darcheville scored a classic on the counter after great work from Steven Davis. Then Steven Whittaker went crazy on the field and believed he was Messi. He slalomed the length of the field past five defenders before slotting home. Jim Beglin on commentary chuckled and said, 'Was he supposed to do that?' (interestingly, most fans I knew watched the ITV4 coverage and the English coverage rather than the STV coverage. There's just something inherently shit about STV sport). We won 2–0 and were through to the semis.

Domestically, we annoyed the whole country by not losing to Dundee United in the League Cup Final. United chairman Eddie Thompson was suffering from cancer and was said to have little time left. The papers focused on this aspect of the match in the build-up. United were by far the better team and led with a few minutes to go. They felt they had been denied a clear penalty in the second half, which gave their charmless manager Craig Levein something to whine about. Then their midfielder, Mark Kerr, inexplicably knocked the ball straight to Kris Boyd for the equaliser. United led in extra-time but Boyd equalised again. In the penalty shoot-out, Lee Wilkie missed a crucial kick for United and Boyd, of course, dispatched his for the win. It was hard not to feel sympathy for Thompson, but the first leg of an unlikely quadruple had been achieved.

The season was now a heady rush. It was like being a teenager again, the prospect of the new, the intense joy of so many novel experiences. We welcomed Italian cracks Fiorentina to Ibrox for the UEFA Cup semi-final. In a match that was simply overwhelmed with tension, we drew 0–0. I must admit I thought the game was up at this point. A penalty shoot-out victory over St Johnstone had put us in the Scottish Cup Final against lowly Queen of the South. The League title had seemed a certainty when a Kevin Thomson goal gave us a 1–0 win over Celtic at Ibrox, but in the next match at Parkhead, Celtic triumphed 2–1 in an incredible match, scoring a sickening 94th-minute winner. This meant we had to play them at Parkhead again in a crucial match. The reason for two matches being played back to back at Parkhead was that Celtic had requested that the January match be postponed after the shocking and tragic death of Phil O'Donnell, the Motherwell captain. O'Donnell had collapsed and died during a match against Dundee United. He had played for Celtic a decade earlier and it was because of this that they requested the postponement. Many Rangers fans speculated that their poor form and injury crisis may also have had a fair bit to do with this as only one Celtic player had actually played with O'Donnell. It did seem excessive that out of all other Scottish teams, only Celtic were so traumatised that they were given a postponement. Dundee United had been involved in the match where the tragedy had taken place and they were not granted a postponement. Only the powerbrokers at Celtic will know what their rationale was for this, though they wheeled out their apologists in the media to justify it. If it was due to any other reason than grief, you question how these people sleep at night. Hugh Keevins said anybody who could even suggest that there were other motives for the postponement was a sick individual, but this was from a man who compared fans attending a football match with the flag of their nation to Nazis attending one of Hitler rallies, so he can be ignored.

The second leg rolled around. Rangers fought for their lives. Let's be honest, Fiorentina were the better side and gave us a bit of a doing, but they couldn't score. I was watching in a pub in Shawlands, pretty much just expecting the goal that would signal our exit. The longer it went on, the more hopeful I became, while simultaneously more dreading the inevitable kick in the stones. Fiorentina brought on the 68-year-old Christian Vieri, who proceeded to miss an open goal from under the bar. Daniel Cousin nutted an opposition player and got sent off. My heart was now resembling a highly-strung cocaine addict after some exciting news. We held on for penalties. I turned to Scot and said, 'This is just too cruel. I'd rather have just gone out 2–0 than this.' Ferguson stepped up to hit our first and missed. Bugger. The Fiorentina player who followed scored his penalty then gave a dismissive 'flicking dandruff off his collar' gesture to signify how it had been too easy. Such unexpected penalty takers as Brahim Hemdani, Sasa Papac and Steven Whittaker slotted calmly away for us. Then our reserve 'keeper, Neil Alexander, in because of injury to McGregor, saved a Fiorentina attempt. Nacho Novo ran up to take what could be the decisive penalty. Anyone else would be nervous, but not wee Nacho. He sprinted up, desperate to be the hero. Peter Drury uttered the immortal line as Nacho stepped up, 'Brace yourself, Manchester,' – Nacho scored – 'because Rangers are coming!' It was bedlam in the pub. People in Glasgow streets jumped, sang and cried. I went out until 5am, walking around like a lottery winner on acid. The realisation immediately hit me – I was going. I had a hotel room and two tickets. I was going to Manchester. I was suddenly very popular with my friends.

The recipient of my second ticket was my Dad. It was always going to be my Dad, though Scot put in a half-arsed attempt. But this was a wee chance to pay my Dad back a little for all the love. If I had my time again and got to pick my parents, I'd pick the same two. He was over the moon. It meant we were spared the ungodly ticket scramble. Supply could never meet demand. It was being held at Eastlands, Manchester City's 44,000 capacity stadium. Travel club members were sorted first, then season ticket holders. Stephen paid £600 online for two. Scot panicked a fair bit, and a few toys were thrown on FF, but he eventually ended up with two. This led to a couple of incidents that made me proud to be a Rangers fan. Iain M. was awarded one ticket in the ballot, and immediately gave it to his then-

16-year-old son, Stuart. What a fantastic thing to do. I wouldn't have. On hearing this, Scot gave his spare ticket to Iain. That's what being a Bear is all about. Those two gestures made me very proud of my friends.

The press in Scotland didn't seem as excited as we were. If we sang a naughty song in a match away to Inverness, my phone was like Batman's in summer, but now my team was in a European Final, plans were afoot for a mass invasion and only the BBC, the *Record* and Real Radio seemed interested. The *News of the World* had two columnists, Davie Provan and Gerry McNee, neither of whom could bring themselves to congratulate us the week we went through or wish us luck the week before the game. Indeed, so blatant were their attempts to ignore it and hope it would just go away, it moved Bill Leckie in their sister paper, *The Sun,* to comment on it. Jim Traynor mentioned in both the *Daily Record* and his BBC show that the Scottish media seemed less enthused by Rangers' Final than they had for Celtic's.

The build-up continued. Our League form really did drop off. We lost 3–2 at Parkhead thanks to a dodgy penalty, but no one cared. We were still favourites for the League, but fixtures began piling up. We asked for an extension to the season. Celtic argued against this, claiming it would damage the 'sporting integrity' of the League, and that they'd already booked a trip to Japan. They didn't remember to go on this trip once the season finished. In the end the SPL didn't help us, and they announced that we'd play four games in seven days after the Final. Would this have happened to any other club in Scotland? No chance.

A chap from the *Manchester Evening News* called me the week before the game and said how excited the city was about the game. He told me the police were estimating that up to 30,000 Bears could travel. 'Aye, on the Monday!' I said. He was stunned when I told him there would be well over 100,000. The police, he said, were not prepared for this. We called them, but they were adamant: fans without tickets should not travel. I warned them that this was akin to standing in the ocean demanding that the water didn't get your feet wet.

We decided to drive down on the day of the game. Convoys were leaving Glasgow for a few days before. Scot and I stayed with my parents the night before the game, and on the train on the way to my parents' house, a Tim in his 50s gave us dirty looks all the way down the line. When he got off at the stop before, he gave us two fingers. I almost pissed myself laughing. We were up at 4am to depart for Manchester the next day. When we hit the motorway at 5am it was already packed with Rangers fans. All the cars had scarves and flags flying. It was astonishing. Everywhere you looked was a sea of blue. Radio 2 travel news basically said, 'Go and see this if you can.' I will never forget it as long as I live. Even then, it was only a precursor for what we saw when we got into Manchester at 11am. There were Rangers fans everywhere. Any street you turned down, any road you walked, any shop you went into, there were thousands and thousands of us, like a red, white and blue tsunami. Still they kept coming from every part of the country. It got incredibly, overwhelmingly busy. We, thank the Lord, had a hotel. The room we had turned out to be a triple so Scot got booked in for £30. People were paying £500 for a room.

Follow Follow were running an event in a Manchester nightclub, which we went along to. I met Simon, who told me he'd shaved his balls the night before and was regretting it now. Not as much as I was regretting shaking his hand, I told him. Ian B. and Tommy B. were there. Ian was sweating on a ticket. Before he got it, he resembled a Bear with a sore head. He was about ready to blow the joint up when a ticket was secured. I didn't fancy spending this beautiful sunny day in a dark nightclub so we decided to hit the road. We went to Piccadilly Square. I have no words for this. It was just a sea of red, white and blue. There were already drink casualties. A young lady was lying on the ground, passed out and legs akimbo. I got a copper and pointed her out. We didn't linger long at the big screens — once we'd seen the people, I wanted to go for a pint. Every bar in Manchester was packed. I then had an idea.

If you know Manchester, you may know Canal Street, its thriving gay district. I decided we should try there. It was a sight indeed, a curious mixture of football fans and flamboyant homosexuals. We ended up in a bar called Queer. The regulars were incredibly friendly, and the Bears were happy to have a seat and a beer. The meeting of these tribes had me in tears of laughter a few times. The gay patrons decided they would use the ladies' toilet to prevent any embarrassment to the newcomers. As I was walking down the stairs to use the gents, a chap veered left into the ladies. A wee 'Gers fan in front said 'Mate, that's the wrong one. That's the women's.' The chap replied, 'Oh, I know, love, I just don't want you feeling awkward.' The fan grabbed him and pulled him towards the bog saying, 'Ah, for f**ksake, big man, it's not like you've never seen a cock before.' My Dad isn't a big drinker and wanted to move on to tea. The bar didn't sell tea, so the staff made him in a cup from their kitchen. A wee Bear approached the bar staff to see if they were showing the game. No, they said, they didn't show sports. A big guy, who resembled Christopher Biggins, chastised the barman and told him to show the game for the boys. They ended up doing so, and the pub was packed to the rafters. I'm pretty sure a few Rangers fans had new experiences that night.

We were playing Zenit St Petersburg, managed by Dick Advocaat. They were better than us. I actually knew a fair bit about them because my friend Gerry's wife is from St Petersburg, and we'd been to Moscow and her hometown on holiday the year before. They were backed by Gazprom and had some fabulous players. It was going to be a tough match. Their star player was a wee chap called Andrei Arshavin. He would take some stopping. I actually own a Zenit top but decided not to wear it that day!

At about 6pm we headed up to the ground. I'll never forget it. The walk was astonishing. There were thousands and thousands of Bears. We met loads of people we knew, and then we were there. They were checking every ticket individually though, and it took us half an hour to get in. As if we weren't tense enough beforehand. Getting in with five minutes to spare, we had second-tier, halfway line tickets. Perfect. I gave my old man a hug and we settled down to watch it. We played OK. We didn't go for it, which is a regret. While the atmosphere was incredible, we were cagey and looked like we were going for a win on penalties. Arshavin slipped a wonderful ball through and we were a goal down. We chased it but never really looked like getting a goal. They got a second in injury time, and we'd lost. There were no complaints, the better team won.

There were reports of trouble in the city centre. We woke to visceral images of police being attacked by Rangers fans. They'd made the decision to turn off the big screen in Piccadilly Square before the game started, and it had kicked off. Although there was only a minute percentage of the 200,000 Bears involved – police estimated about 300 – it looked awful. The images that played around the world included a frightening incident where a policeman looked in danger of his life. It was an awful ending to a wonderful trip. The recriminations started immediately. I utterly condemned the actions of the idiots and thugs but stated one salient point: they weren't getting to steal my day from me. These halfwits couldn't stain the day I, and thousands of Bears, had had.

Disconsolately, we headed into our next few League matches. We drew with Motherwell before beating St Mirren. This meant we had to win away to Aberdeen and hope Celtic lost at Dundee United. We lost and they won, so they captured the title. They had to win 13 games in a row to win the League, and they did so. Congratulations to them. We then had the Scottish Cup Final to contest. I have never known an atmosphere like it. The 'Gers fans were sullen. The message seemed to be 'just win this and wave the trophy at us so we can go and celebrate'. The team duly did, winning 3–2 after letting a 2–0 lead slip. An extraordinary campaign was over.

I now knew what Celtic fans meant when they said they wouldn't have traded 2003 for anything. Manchester was a wonderful experience and I was proud of having been a part of it. We'd finished with two trophies and had some memories to last us a lifetime. Everyone was knackered, though. We all needed a break from football.

We Deserve Better

We simply had to win the League in 2008–09. The season started appallingly. Having not spent on any midfielders, we went into a Champions League qualifier against minnows Kaunas of Lithuania. We drew 0–0 at home with a midfield including Lee McCulloch and Christian Dailly. Then, shockingly, we lost 2–1 over there, going from a European Final to European humiliation in two months. It was a surprising result and a dereliction of duty by the club to think we could 'get by' with the players we had. It cost us much-needed revenue, which was to have a massive effect on us. The failure to bring in any midfielders was rectified by the signings of Pedro Mendes from Portsmouth and the permanent transfer of Steven Davis from Fulham, but it was a case of shutting the stable door after the horse had not only bolted, but set up home in another country. The depression was further enhanced by the sale of star defender Carlos Cuellar. He had a clause in his contract that meant the club had to let him go for an agreed fee of just under £8 million. This meant we were shorn of our best player and out of Europe. We'd also signed Kenny Miller, a deeply unpopular move. People hadn't forgotten his time at Celtic.

The Trust changed, too. A group of seven board members left. I suspect they thought the Trust would implode. An article appeared in the *Daily Record* to that effect. In actuality, the departures had no significant impact, as the people who left were no great losses. The members who were irreplaceable – people like Simon Leslie, Mark Dingwall, Stephen Smith, Christine Sommerville and the incomparable Joanne Percival – remained.

Solace arrived in the form of a spectacular 4–2 win at Parkhead. Mendes scored a belter, and Artur Boruc made an arse of himself by dropping the ball at Miller's feet, allowing the striker to score the second of his brace. This went some way to helping him win over the many sceptics. We were seven points ahead at this point, but this was eroded by Christmas. After this match came one of those Celtic-launched initiatives that always seem to take place when we've beaten them soundly. The 'Gers fans had taken to singing 'Why don't you go home, the famine's over' to mock Celtic and their perceived Irishness. This was mainly directed at Aiden McGeady, a Scotsman who'd chosen to play (often badly) for the Republic of Ireland. A massive media storm erupted, which knocked the result off the pages. Celtic chairman Dr John Reid, the former Home Secretary, said the song was racist. Reid, unpopular with his fans for his part in the invasion of Iraq in 2003, was doing what career politicians do: grandstanding. My view on it is clear. Someone with his past is in no position to be lecturing people on anything to do with morals. I think there are a lot of worse things in the world than this song – he caused some of them. As for the song, it's offensive, but it is meant to be. That's the whole point of it. Unpleasant? Yes. Racist? No.

It's like the deeply unsavoury 'Big Jock Knew' chants at Ibrox. This is in reference to the Celtic Boys Club scandal, when youth players were sexually abused by a coach called Jim Torbett. It's a pretty seedy part of Celtic's history, which they understandably shy away from. Torbett was kicked out of the club after these allegations in the 1960s but was not charged until to the 1990s. At his trial, it was suggested Jock Stein, the manager at the time, knew about the abuse but failed to report it to the police (Celtic, to their shame, continued to accept money from Torbett's business). Rangers fans sing this to annoy Celtic fans, who rightly deify their European Cup-winning manager. Is child abuse an acceptable thing to taunt your rivals about? No. My sympathy is somewhat limited though. It is difficult to accept these complaints from a support who revelled in singing about Richard Gough being a child molester in the early 1990s, despite this being a complete fabrication. But it is an awful chant which does us no favours and should cease.

A defeat to Celtic at Ibrox left us seven points behind in January. Then came the news that Rangers had to sell a player to help balance the books. Top scorer Kris Boyd was being touted to Birmingham for £4 million. The fans were outraged. We decided the time was right to ask major questions of the club. We did this in a document entitled 'We Deserve Better'.

This was a banner flown by The Blue Order in the wake of Kaunas, which seemed to sum up the feelings of the fan. I sent out the following press release:

RANGERS SUPPORT LAUNCH 'WE DESERVE BETTER' CAMPAIGN

The Rangers support have shown our loyalty time and time again, culminating in a world-record 200,000 supporters travelling to Manchester for the UEFA Cup Final in May 2008. This is an achievement no other club in the world could match. Our loyal supporters have, however, grown increasingly frustrated at the direction the club has taken in the last decade, with a pattern of events showing that the Board of Rangers FC have failed the support consistently.

Areas of concern include:
- Only 2 League titles in 8 seasons;
- Only 2 Cups won in last 3 full seasons;
- Losing to the worst European opponents faced since Valletta in 1983;

- A 'state of the art' training facility, yet no advancements in technique or set plays;
- No discernible strategic vision, either on or off the pitch;
- No long-term transfer or team-building plan;
- Only two youth players (McGregor and Hutton) of genuine quality produced in the last decade;
- Selling first-team players to cover losses previously made on fringe players;
- Consistent failure to move fringe players on for reasonable transfer fees;
- Lucrative pay-offs for failed players;
- Failure to profit from our most lucrative ever season;
- Failure to engage with or interact with the support in any meaningful way;
- Treating Rangers fans with disdain as 'customers' instead of valuing and working with them as 'supporters' and part of the Rangers family;
- Inability to either attract inward investment or to convince fans to invest in any meaningful way;
- Reduction in the status of our club from leading football force in the land, to almost 'social pariah' status through a failure to challenge those seeking to link Rangers with sectarianism;
- A PR operation which only acts when senior club figures are personally criticised and all too often fails to defend the Rangers support;
- Fan morale lower than at any time in the past 24 years.

We deserve better.
- We have always been the club who set the standards for others to follow.
- It was Rangers who led the way in stadium redevelopment. It was Rangers who dragged Scottish football forward by signing

big-name English and European players. Other teams trailed in our wake.

- There is so much to be grateful for that we are Rangers fans. Right now, however, our current regime is not even aspiring to the standards set by their predecessors.

We deserve better.

- We now issue a public challenge to the Board of the club to take steps which will improve our situation immediately, to state what they plan to do and to work with the support.
- Rangers fans do understand that the current situation will take time and a workable strategy to escape from, but the club must make the major changes necessary rather than conduct transfer window fire-sales and lurch from crisis to crisis with no discernible game plan.

We deserve better.

- We call on all fans' groups and supporters to unite to let the club Board know how we feel. While we will continue to back the team 100 per cent, as is the way of Rangers fans, the people at the top of the club must realise that we will no longer accept the avoidable situation we currently find ourselves in.

We deserve better.

- It's time for the club Board to recognise this and strive to achieve it.

Well, the shit hit the fan, let me tell you. The club went on the attack, calling us malcontents and launching a full-on assault on me personally. I was criticised in the media, I was called a gloryhunter, and I was cited as the reason for things actually being wrong with the club! Many backed us, but a lot didn't. I received death threats, this time serious, and, worst of all, this time from Bears. I was used to angry Celtic fans, but this was the first time I had received it from fellow 'Gers. Things got hairy. The thing was, the club didn't respond to any of the points in the actual document. Murray spoke about the recession but conveniently forgot to mention that we'd been in the shit while the rest of the world was apparently booming. I started getting nuisance calls. Stuff arrived in the post, graphically depicting what would happen to me if I didn't shut my mouth. Chic Young, on instruction from his higher-up, called me all manner of nasty things. It wasn't nice for my parents or wife to hear and made me question why I was doing this.

In the early days, I loved the attention. I'm not going to lie. But after a while it really started to pale. I couldn't go out without fear of some idiot starting on me. I'd been verbally abused while out with my wife. I'd been lambasted in the papers. I didn't need it. Remember, I was doing all this as a volunteer. People couldn't understand why I was putting myself through it. At the end of the day, when I analysed it, it came down to one thing: I loved my club. I wanted them to be better. The points in that statement are valid. They needed answers.

Things picked up, and we ended up winning the League with a superb last-day win over Dundee United. Some people asked how I felt now. Did I feel stupid? Not at all. All of the statement was vindicated. Boyd wasn't sold and went on to be a vital part in our success. I stood up for what I believed in. And as for how I felt – I was a Rangers fan and we'd just won the League – I was ecstatic!

That summer, though, my life fell apart. I lost my job, split up from my wife and suffered a breakdown. The constant stress definitely had an effect. When you are getting home scared of what's in the post, and when your phone rings and you have a panic attack at the prospect of what is coming, you live on your nerves. After 17 years of pretty hard drinking, I realised I had to give up or I was going to die. That's not an exaggeration. It was that clear. The doctor looked at my weekly units and shook his head. Suddenly all the things that had been important didn't seem so vital. I had been running at 100 miles an hour for years, and I couldn't do it any more. **189**

My body was battered and my head was sore. I was so busy trying to fix everything else, I found I hadn't bothered with me. You can run at that pace for a while, but one day you will hit the wall, and that's what happened to me. Spiritually, my gas was at a peep. There was a slight flicker from the pilot light, but that was it.

As the new season started I offered my resignation. I was talked out of it. The club was in peril. Walter announced in October that Lloyds Bank was running the club. I did my mouthpiece bit for the Trust and tried to rally the troops as best I could. We attempted to secure investment for a fans' buy-out. David Murray put the club up for sale, but no bidders made a concrete offer. There was talk of a London property developer called Andrew Ellis buying the club, but after months of speculation he didn't. Where were we going? I do believe the fans owning the club is the way forward. Chairmen, managers and players come and go, but we are there for life. It works at many European clubs. The RST ran a conference where we had speakers from Hamburg and Espanyol suggesting ways to run the club as fans. It is very doable.

Walter did astonishingly well with the team, helped by a pathetic performance from Celtic manager Tony Mowbray, who spent all season taking bad results on the chin until he was sacked following a 4–0 defeat by relegation-haunted St Mirren. We beat the Saints in a remarkable Final, Kenny Miller scoring the winning goal when we were down to nine men after two red cards. We romped to the League title, securing Champions League football for a second successive season and helping ensure the very future of the club. This was Walter's definitive triumph. He hadn't been able to sign a player in two years. He had one hand tied behind his back and he hammered the opposition.

Celtic made an arse of themselves this season by claiming that it was all down to nasty officials and that every decision was being awarded to us. A 'senior' figure at the club even leaked this to the press. It backfired and caused Celtic to be laughed at by anyone neutral. I'm not saying we don't get decisions, but for Celtic to claim they don't beggars belief.

I was finally able to leave the Trust at the 2010 AGM. I'd had a good run. I'm now sober, happy and settled. I had grown tired of never talking about the actual football. For years, all I seemed to talk about was sectarianism, takeovers, chairmen and off-the-field problems. I wanted to talk about who goes best with whom in midfield, whom our best striker was and why referees are bastards. I needed to just be a fan. People were always criticising me for presuming to speak on behalf of the support. I can only apologise. I have no regrets, though. I have been to places I'd never have been and done things I'd never have done. I've genuinely helped tackle actual sectarianism. I've sat with a Rangers chairman and shaped the future of the club. I've been involved in discussions about when a manager should leave. Best of all, I've met hundreds, if not thousands of Rangers fans, and I love being one of them. They make me feel proud of who and what I am. I'm one of them.

When I started this, all I wanted was to be able to say that I did my best for Rangers. I really do believe I achieved that. The Trust presented me with a beautiful crystal vase on my retirement. As well as thanking me for my hard work, it also included this quote from Oscar Wilde (who I think was a Tim, by the way): 'We are all in the gutter, but some of us are looking at the stars.' I like that. Rangers should never settle, should never be just another club. We always have to strive to be better. This is who we are, this is what we do. I was born a Ranger and I'll die one, and I couldn't be happier.

In closing, the one unequivocal, one unarguable fact: We are the people. I'm just proud I'm one of them.